BEAT THE SYSTEM

BOOKS BY ROBERT W. MACDONALD

Cheat to Win: The Honest Way to Break All the Dishonest Rules in Business

Control Your Future: A Candid Guide to Successful Life Insurance Selling

BEAT THE SYSTEM

11 Secrets to Building an Entrepreneurial Culture in a Bureaucratic World

Robert W. MacDonald

John Wiley & Sons, Inc.

Library of Congress Cataloging-in-Publication Data:
MacDonald, Robert W.
    Beat the system : 11 secrets to building an entrepreneurial culture in a bureaucratic world / Robert W. MacDonald.
      p. cm.
    Includes bibliographical references and index.
    ISBN 978-0-470-17549-1 (cloth : alk. paper)
    1. Entrepreneurship—United States.   2. Bureaucracy—United States.   I. Title.
HB615.M316   2008
658.4'21—dc22
                                                                    2007016898

Printed in the United States of America
10 9 8 7 6 5 4 3 2 1

*This book is dedicated to each and every one
of the individuals who supported me
in my quest for success. All of these individuals
populate this book and without them
it would not have been possible.*

Contents

Preface

The image of America and *being* an American has had, for more than 200 years, an almost mystical attraction for people the world over. The very idea of America and of being an American has exuded a magic that supersedes all known geographical or cultural limits. The Irish farmer, the Italian cobbler, the Chinese laborer, and the Indian fakir all had one thing in common—the dream of becoming an American.

The United States offered a unique appeal to people that has remained fairly constant since our country emerged as a nation of immigrants. Being an American has been associated with the dream of achieving religious freedom, economic prosperity, and opportunity.

While common perceptions of the United States are often framed in terms of American capitalism and the freedoms guaranteed by the U.S. Bill of Rights, newcomers to this country speak of freedom, opportunity, and a new way of life available in this land of plenty. Small wonder that millions have risked life and limb in an effort to come to the United States and become an American citizen in a land that welcomed these immigrants with open arms:

Give me your tired, your poor, your huddled masses yearning to breathe free, the wretched refuse of your teeming shore. Send these, the homeless, tempest-tost to me, I lift my lamp beside the golden door!

These words emblazoned on the Statue of Liberty must have brought tears to the eyes of millions of immigrants yearning to be Americans promising, as it did, that they could share in the financial security, material comfort, and better life this country offers, free from social, ethnic, or class boundaries.

Now, fast-forward to the United States of today and you'll discover that there is another dream that beckons individuals every bit as energetically as the vision of America that attracted millions of immigrants to leave the security of a familiar homeland to search for a new life. It drives thousands of people each year to risk all they have acquired and achieved in order to live the concept. This dream is the vibrant desire to become an *entrepreneur*.

Much like the American immigrants of the past who left unhappy lives in their homelands and took unimaginable risks to achieve a happier, new life in the United States, the new "immigrants" seek to escape the predictable doldrums of the *business* world—the system, if you will—and start their own businesses. They see the system of business as practiced by most of the United States as a powerful controlling factor in their lives from which they wish to escape, often desperately so.

Being an entrepreneur in the United States is seen as the last frontier of the American dream, the yellow-brick road to riches. But more importantly, entrepreneurism offers the opportunity to control your own destiny. And it seems that everyone wants to hitch his or her dreams to the concept of "being your own boss," of telling the bureaucratic business world to "take this job and shove it."

Sadly, many try, but most fail. And that's because very few people really understand what it means to be an entrepreneur, let alone how to become a successful one. And we can easily see why.

Ask any group of people how many want to be an entrepreneur and most hands will go up. But ask the same group to give you one word that would epitomize the entrepreneurial concept and you will hear sundry definitions that elude precise quantifiable meaning. Words like *visionary*, and *risk taker* frequently pop up, as well as *leader, innovator, independent,* and even *greedy.*

Whatever the vision, ask many of those stuck in seemingly dead-end jobs at companies festering with bureaucracy what they'd most likely want to do (if they could) and virtually all of them will tell you they want to be an entrepreneur. But why is this?

Most would-be entrepreneurs yearn to be outside the business system under which they experience great frustration with little satisfaction and few rewards. In fact, being viewed as "outside the system" seems to be one of the perks of the entrepreneurial lifestyle, a powerful magnet attracting rank-and-file employees to escape the herd. They have concluded that the only way to "beat the system" is to leave the system, become an entrepreneur, and start a business of their own.

I certainly understand how people feel because I have felt that way most of my life. However, I was fortunate enough to discover the secrets to being a successful entrepreneur: in fact, 11 simple secrets that enabled me to chart a course to an entrepreneurial life and freedom from business bureaucracy. Not that I was able to banish bureaucrats and bureaucracy from my life (that would be like living without taxes), but I did learn how to limit the bureaucracy in my life. My theory of entrepreneurialism contains most of the traditional elements people associate with being an entrepreneur, but my experience leads me to a broader concept of being entrepreneurial.

Being in business for yourself does not necessarily make you an entrepreneur. There are numerous reasons why businesses fail, but I believe that the number one reason is because the owner is not a true entrepreneur, and worse, doesn't know how to become one. I also believe you don't have to "strike out on your own" to be an entrepreneur. My experience has taught me that being an employee for even the largest corporation does not preclude one from being entrepreneurial.

Sure, it is great to go out on your own and start a company—
I did it and would encourage doing so in the right environment. But
becoming an entrepreneur and earning the benefits does not require
that you go outside the system. You must simply *beat* the system.

So what is the "system" anyway? And, why would we want to
"beat" it? The first step to building an entrepreneurial culture is to recognize that we live in a bureaucratic world. (As if we didn't know
that!) Bureaucracy *is* the system. And if the goal is to push our business
careers and personal lives to the pinnacle of success, we are going to
have to beat the system that is dedicated to preventing us from doing
so. We have to escape from the system that binds, deadens, and calci-
fies our ability to achieve the success that we define. The only way to
do that is to adopt an entrepreneurial spirit in everything we do.

Having made that decision, you'll soon discover that the system
works against your attempts to break free. You will find that those in
charge of the system do everything in their power to maintain the
status quo, to keep you walking the straight line. The system discourages the vast majority of people from even trying. And when that
does happen, those in charge win by default.

The first thing you have to accept is that it is okay to beat the
system. Then the critical issue is to understand how to beat the system the correct way—the honest way. Much of the business world
wants us to believe that when we try to beat the system, we are doing
something wrong. The defining issue is being able to distinguish the
difference between attempting to beat the system the dishonest way
and beating it the honest way by innovating to create an entrepreneurial culture.

This book gives you a practical, realistic guide to achieving the
real benefits of being an entrepreneur. It could mean striking out to
start your own business, but it could also mean learning how to be
more entrepreneurial, and therefore, more successful, within a larger
organization. As part of the process, you learn how to fight off

bureaucracy, break the back of the bureaucrat, and, in fact, change the system.

Beat the System is written for business managers, owners, employees, and entrepreneurs who seek to create and perpetuate that powerful entrepreneurial élan that generates success on all levels, both personal and professional. If you're content with the status quo, with a paycheck twice a month for putting in your dues, this book is *not* for you.

My primary audience for this book is neophyte entrepreneurs who are starting (or want to start) a business. It will help them build an entrepreneurial culture that will not only prosper—but will be *resistant* to the corrosive effects of bureaucratic regimes that will wittingly ooze into their business fabric. And believe me, they will try.

Moreover, since bureaucracy is everywhere, all throughout your business life you'll constantly be fighting with this menace. Surprisingly, few have sought to teach us how to successfully beat bureaucracy. Certainly schools don't teach us how to beat the system—for the most part, they epitomize the system. Few books have attempted to tackle the subject. My hope is that this book can be your survival manual for living in a bureaucratic world.

Beat the System is also written for executives who have become leaders of a business that is struggling, not just to thrive but to *survive*. An opportunity for a corporate entrepreneurial rebirth occurs when a major management shakeup is performed to rescue a failing company. This happens in business all the time, but unfortunately, all too often the "makeover" consists of hiring a new staff of technocrats who infuse the dying company with even more bureaucratic nonsense. That needn't happen. This book and its 11 simple secrets shows you how to imbue even the most entrenched bureaucracy with a fresh, new entrepreneurial soul.

And finally—maybe most importantly—this book is written for those who are still in the formative stages of building a career. Those who are not yet sure where the road before them will lead, but who want to give themselves every opportunity to be successful. I am hopeful this book will help younger employees and those working their way up in an organization (or seeking escape) to avoid the dark side where sluggish growth and rule-mania abound. This book will help you create a career that sparkles with ingenuity and success.

I realize there are some who will argue that entrepreneurial change can only come about with a change at the top, and to a certain degree, I agree with that assessment. Major corporate change invariably springs from the front office and percolates throughout the organization—if that is management's intention. But by no means do I agree with the notion that individual managers and employees can't be entrepreneurial in their approach to their jobs. They certainly can, and this book shows you how.

Again, nobody said it's going to be easy. In fact, it's likely to be difficult, regardless of your position, whether business owner, corporate executive, manager, or interoffice gofer. But, you can beat the system—if you really want to.

The critical step is recognizing the system for what it is and how it seeks to control and limit your future. Then, once you know the enemy and its treacherous ways, you become willing to take the action needed to implement the techniques necessary to build an entrepreneurial culture that can thwart and beat the system. The key is to start now—don't wait. The system is getting stronger every day. The longer you wait, the more difficult it will be to beat it. Nolan Bushnell, the entrepreneur who founded Atari, could not have offered better advice to a would-be entrepreneur when he said, "The critical thing is to get off your butt and do something. And the time to do it is not tomorrow, and not next week. The true entrepreneur is a doer, not a dreamer."

You can beat the system by adopting an entrepreneurial spirit and by building your entrepreneurial culture right now. This book can help make that goal a reality.

Acknowledgments

It has been my good fortune to have experienced a long, varied, and what most would agree has been a successful business career. Moving from college dropout to a leader of multibillion dollar corporations is not what many would have expected as I entered the business world in 1965. Yet, the record is there. Why? Only because along the way, I was fortunate enough to encounter a large number of individuals who seemed to take as much interest in my advancement as I did and who worked hard to support my efforts. This was not a calculated plan, but for some reason it happened.

How do you thank those who sublimate their personal interests for yours? The only thing I could think of at the time was to share as much of the success as possible because it was not really my success. The result has been a 40-year accumulation of individuals who are the real reason for any success I have enjoyed.

When it comes to the specifics of producing this book, I want to acknowledge and thank Charles (Chuck) Wetherall. Chuck, who was vital to the development of my previous book *Cheat to Win* (Minneapolis, MN: Paradon Publishing, 2005) continued to encourage, contribute, challenge, correct, and prod me as this book moved forward. Chuck has been the hand behind the scene who kept things moving, focused, and on schedule. If you enjoy this book, it is because Chuck's efforts made it better than I could ever have done. For that I thank him.

Prologue: A Case Study for Beating the System

At most business schools, the favored technique for teaching young future business leaders is called the *case method*. The logic of this system, as I understand it (I'm not sure because I was never admitted to any business school), is that if students read books full of case studies about company failures and successes, they'll develop the perspicacity to lead the future businesses they manage down a road free from those dreaded potholes. I guess it must work since the business schools have been using it for years.

As students review these cases, they discover a number of key issues that must be surmounted if a business is to be successful. Most of these obstacles could be included in what is generally referred to as *barriers to entry*. Students learn that if barriers to entry are too high, it's simply foolish to buck the known evidence by starting a business.

Some of the traditional barriers to entry include:

- The industry you wish to enter is mature or stagnant.
- The competition in the industry is sufficiently large so as to prohibit a level playing field.

- The products or services in this industry are routine and undifferentiated. (Who needs another milk producer?)
- Capital requirements for entry are large and formidable.
- Ongoing capital needs are so ravenous as to prevent funding the venture.
- The industry is highly regulated by government or has quasi-governmental control.

Now, let's do one of our own case studies. We'll use the U.S. life insurance industry as a model. Your assignment is to study the insurance industry and determine whether you would recommend this industry as meaty new ground for your business. For extra credit, you are welcome to submit white papers describing the chances for such a business success.

The starting point of your homework is to first examine the established barriers to entry in the life insurance industry. Here's what you'll find:

- The U.S. life insurance industry is the largest in the world. Annual sales are measured in hundreds of billions of dollars and assets under management are counted in the trillions. In short, they have a considerable war chest to crush any new competitors should they find it necessary and desirable to do so.
- The U.S. life insurance industry is a mature (some would say mundane) industry. A few insurance companies have been doing business since Abigail Adams was throwing tea parties in the White House. Moreover, for the past 40 years, total industry growth has been stagnant. Sure, existing companies have grown, but the percentage of consumer dollars allocated to the life insurance industry has been in steady decline. This means that the growing companies are simply taking a bigger piece of a smaller pie. That is a barrier for any new company entering the market.

- Is the industry growing? Nope. In 1960, there were over 2,000 operating life insurance companies in the United States. By the 1990s, this number had dwindled to just a few hundred. And it was not just the small companies that exited the business. Some of the oldest and largest companies were unable to compete in this stagnant market and either went out of business or were sold or merged with other companies. As a result, the insurance industry is dominated by the very largest and most established companies.

- While the U.S. life insurance industry has never had a reputation for innovation and creativity in product offerings, regulatory issues and the dominance of the large companies meant that for most of the twentieth century all companies sold virtually the same products at the same price. Insurance policies were as indistinguishable as shampoos or hair conditioners at a suburban mall. This virtually seals off the industry from any new entry by a company selling another "me-too" product.

- When it comes to need for capital, the life insurance industry is rather unique. It is highly capital intensive but in a most unusual way. Most industries require capital to get started, but once up and running with product being sold, the need for capital shrinks. Life insurance companies face a double-whammy. They need capital to support the policies they issue, but profits won't show up for several years after the policy is issued. In short, the faster your company grows, the more capital it requires. Since capital is the most difficult and expensive item for any new company to acquire, the requirement for high levels of capital in the insurance industry serves as a huge and effective barrier to entry for new companies.

- The life insurance industry is one of the most heavily regulated industries in the United States. All products offered by the companies must be individually approved by government bureaucrats in each and every state. To make their job easier, states enact a gauntlet of regulations within which each policy must pass. Such a system inhibits (if not actually makes impossible) the development of innovative products.

Talk about a regulatory nightmare. This obviously favors the status quo. Established companies are running the insurance industry show and that raises a formidable barrier for any new company or product. And if that's not bad enough, each state has the right to scrutinize the financial credibility and strength of each company. If they're not satisfied, they can prohibit the company from issuing policies. Period.

- There is another unique and very high barrier to entry into the life insurance industry. Since life insurance companies offer products that promise to protect or enhance the financial future of the consumer, the financial reputation of a company is of critical importance. If the company cannot pay future claims or benefits, other considerations become unimportant.
- Financial strength ratings represent an analysis of a wide variety of risks that could affect an insurer's long-term survival. Insurance companies can fail or cease to operate due to inadequate financial capabilities, competitive forces, or changing fundamentals in their marketplaces.
- Financial ratings are made by organizations such as Standard & Poor's, A.M. Best Co., and others. Without a high financial rating, it is difficult for a company to sell products. This, of course, favors the larger, established companies and is a very high barrier to entry. For the newcomer, it's Catch-22. You've got to have a high rating to attract new business, but you need new business to provide the financial muscle to get a high rating.

- Finally, the life insurance product itself is not one of those hot, impulse products that consumers are eager to buy. You won't find policies stacked neatly on the end-aisles of grocery stores. Insurance products must be sold. Generally, somebody has to knock on your door or pester you on the telephone before you'll buy.

This means your new insurance company venture has to put together an extremely large, persistent (and sometimes obnoxious) distribution system to attain a critical mass of sales. So, chalk up another win for the old, established insurance companies since they have had decades to build distribution.

Okay, now that you have reviewed these barriers to entry in the life insurance industry, would you—in all your business school MBA wisdom—advise someone to invest his life savings in a start-up life insurance company? (Keep your answer clean!) What do you think would be the chances for the success of such a company?

To be honest with you, I would have to agree with most people that you'd have as much chance at successfully starting a new insurance company as ice cream has in surviving a microwave. In fact, most would argue that it is not even possible to start a new life insurance company, let alone become as much as a blip on the business survival radar. And yet, you are reading the book of a guy who was seemingly foolish enough to make such an effort. I say "seemingly" because we had something that the business schools have largely ignored.

I was part of a group that in 1987 started a new life insurance company called LifeUSA. Our objective was to build LifeUSA into a successful national company. Let's see how LifeUSA measured up to the barriers to entry in the life insurance industry:

- LifeUSA was a pure start-up in this mature, slow growth industry that was dominated by large, well-established companies.

- LifeUSA was not able to offer any new or innovative products to differentiate itself from other companies.
- LifeUSA had limited capital and no access to the continuing flow of capital needed for growth.
- LifeUSA was an unknown company with no financial reputation or ratings.
- LifeUSA had absolutely no distribution system to sell its products.

Clearly these limitations would make it virtually impossible for LifeUSA to overcome the barriers to entry in the life insurance industry. So absurd was the idea of a new company entering the life insurance industry that most people could not even comprehend the idea. (Especially those ever-creative risk takers called "bankers." And you know how I feel about bankers. I've got goldfish who are smarter.) People could understand the idea of starting a life insurance *agency* to sell policies, but simply could not fathom the thought of starting a company to actually issue policies.

Yet, despite the handicaps and incongruity of the idea to many, we were able to launch LifeUSA. And what happened?

Surprise! Not only did LifeUSA survive, but it became one of the fastest growing and most successful companies in the life insurance industry. In fact, in the 1990s, LifeUSA became one of the most successful start-up companies in any industry.

After just seven years, LifeUSA had annual sales exceeding $1 billion. Within 10 years, LifeUSA distribution grew to over 85,000 agents. (None of ours were obnoxious. We left the obnoxious ones with the other companies.) LifeUSA became a profitable, publicly traded company in just six years. After only 12 years, LifeUSA assets exceeded $6 billion and financial ratings equaled those of even the largest companies. So successful had LifeUSA become that in 1999 the German company Allianz SE, one of the world's largest financial organizations, offered $540 million to acquire the company.

Not bad for a company with so many high barriers to entry against it that the MBAs pronounced the idea dead on arrival. The irony is that LifeUSA achieved all this success as many of the very largest companies in the industry struggled not only to grow, but to even survive. This naturally leads to the questions: Why and how?

There are at least two reasons for the success of LifeUSA:

1. There was a fundamental change taking place in the industry that the established companies not only failed to recognize, but they stubbornly refused to respond to. And it's not like they didn't have a few thousand actuaries on their staff.

   U.S. life expectancy had risen dramatically since 1900 when many of these old-line insurance companies were formed, largely the result of declining infant and child mortality rates. A baby born today, for example, can expect to live at least *30 years longer* than a baby born at the turn of the century.

   What this new longevity meant was that consumer needs had shifted from fretting about the cost of dying too soon to the cost of living too long. In times of constancy and stability, the big companies will always win, but in times of volatility (which the life insurance was experiencing), it's not the big companies that win but the good companies—the *creative* companies. Of course, big companies can be good companies, but their size makes it difficult for them to respond to change.

2. The most important reason for the success of LifeUSA is due to the fact that the company was built as a purely entrepreneurial culture in an industry awash with bureaucracy. (Actually I would argue for a third reason being exceptional, inspired leadership, but most would reject that idea.) A close examination of LifeUSA reveals that the only difference between LifeUSA and its larger, more established competition was a business model based on entrepreneurial concepts versus

companies that had become dominated by bureaucracy. To be honest, it was no contest!

In the beginning, people would often ask me, "How can you hope to compete against these well-established companies that have dominated the industry for decades?" While not wanting to seem arrogant, I told them they were asking the wrong question. The real question was this: How can these companies possibly compete against LifeUSA? I was comfortable with that response because I knew a secret. And that secret was the awesome power of an entrepreneurial culture over the entrenched bureaucracy. When it was all said and done, entrepreneurialism was the one simple secret to the success of LifeUSA.

And just what were the entrepreneurial secrets imbedded in LifeUSA that created this culture? There are 11. And together they form a bulwark against the kind of thinking, the kind of *behavior* that dooms some businesses from the get-go.

Looking back now 20 years after the founding of LifeUSA, I am even more convinced that the only way we were able to break down the barriers to our success was the implementation, commitment, and internalization of the simple secrets of the entrepreneur.

The entrepreneurial philosophy embodied by the 11 secrets is eminently transferable. You can put this philosophy to work in any management, in any business, at any time, and you don't have to have an MBA to do so.

For example, after Allianz SE acquired our burgeoning LifeUSA in 1999, the company was merged into Allianz Life of North America. Even though Allianz Life was several times larger than LifeUSA, in a decision viewed as unusual, the Germans placed the management of LifeUSA in charge of the merged companies.

We soon discovered the reason for their decision. While Allianz Life was populated with many very talented people, its culture had become enmeshed in bureaucracy and the company was failing. Our challenge was to see if the LifeUSA entrepreneurial culture could be successfully mixed with the bureaucratic culture of Allianz Life. (This effort was complicated because the parent company in Germany was the essence of bureaucracy.)

Yet, the effort worked and worked wonders. When the people of Allianz Life were exposed to the attitude and philosophy of the people of LifeUSA, they opened up and blossomed like spring flowers—the entrepreneurial lifestyle was such a breath of fresh air. (Of course, not all of the Allianz Life people were comfortable with the new philosophy, but most of the very talented ones were.) Once the cultures of LifeUSA and the merged company Allianz Life were combined, the problems of the older Allianz Life were eliminated and the company went on to set even more remarkable records of success.

Why do I bring up LifeUSA? Simple. It gives some credibility to what you are going to read in the following chapters. This is not an armchair philosophy I'm talking about. It's a living, breathing *workable* philosophy that has practical application to your business life, no matter your station.

Becoming a successful entrepreneur in a bureaucratic world is not defined by bucking the odds and starting a company like LifeUSA, but the concepts and principles of LifeUSA do define the entrepreneurial philosophy. The secret is that this philosophy works to create a successful entrepreneurial environment in virtually any situation. By book's end, you'll know how to beat the system—the bureaucratic system that is everywhere about us.

*An entrepreneur is an individual who motivates others
to dedicate themselves to the success of the entrepreneur
because they believe it is in their own best interests to do so.
And it is!*

1

Bureaucracy: The Enemy of Business Success

The system was established to protect the status quo and to discourage individuals from seeking better ways to do things.

If the United States is noted for nothing else, it surely must be credited as a country that has contrived a system for just about everything, from the mundane to the munificent. We have judicial court systems, political systems, and religious systems; we have systems of armed forces, systems of governments, and educational systems. And we have systems that impinge on us on a more personal level, too.

1

Buy gas for your car and you're confronted with a system. Self-serve is the system *de rigueur.* You pull up to the pump, insert your credit card, and pump your own gas (or E-85, but that's another system). If you want to pay in cash, or want to buy a quart of oil, you have to enter through *this* door (not *that* door, that's the exit door), and take the long way around the racks filled with high-margin candy bars, and join a lengthy queue of people buying lottery tickets, the latest issue of *People* magazine, or fishing for 99 cents and a coupon to pay for a 44-ounce "big gulp" soft drink (uh-oh, that's Big Gulp®, yet another system).

That's today's gas station system (and it almost makes you wish those Texaco guys hadn't retired). There is another system waiting for you at the fast-food joint, the place where you renew your drivers' license, at your daughter's school, your drive-in church, your favorite supermarket, the place where you buy eye glasses, and, of course, the business where you work.

Systems Can Be Good for You

With this massive proliferation of systems at all levels of human activity, you'd think that we would be very sophisticated in their use. And generally, I'd agree that we are. Systems are not only necessary in many cases, but downright useful. (And if you don't believe me, try driving northbound on the interstate in the southbound lane.)

Systems make life easier, safer, more uniform, more understandable, and even less expensive to enjoy. If the teenager flipping burgers at a McDonald's in Poughkeepsie had to figure out how to make a Quarter Pounder® with cheese every time he made one, you can be sure it wouldn't taste anything like the one you'd get in Toulouse (besides, as the movie *Pulp Fiction* told us, the French don't eat a Quarter Pounder, they eat a "Royale with Cheese" since the French use the metric system. But that's another system, another story).

The preflight check system used by airline pilots is certainly considered a useful procedure, wouldn't you agree? Without it, there's no telling if other crucial systems are impaired or unworkable. Without it, you might be introduced to a few other systems you might wish to avoid, like the hospital system, the burial system, and the like.

Systems Can Think for Us

Uniform plans, programs, and procedures take much of the independent thinking out of our lives with favorable results. This is particularly true in business. In fact, businesses, second to governments, are the mother lode of systems.

Everywhere you scan the U.S. business landscape, you'll find systems: systems that regulate employee behavior; systems that organize ideas, principles, and doctrines; systems that establish procedures and processes; systems that reduce costs and bring a more established order and harmonious arrangement where otherwise there might be chaos.

If you have a job, any kind of job, you're probably face-to-face with systems of all kinds that largely take over your job of thinking: IT systems. Bookkeeping systems. HR systems. Shipping systems. Payroll systems. Employee manuals. Like it or not, systems like these help make businesses run. Businesses can't survive without them and accordingly, although ruefully, we rarely quibble about their usefulness.

Our systems are useful, as well as pervasive. Systems have diffused our culture to such an extent that we take them for granted in the same way that we expect the light to go on when we throw the switch or cars to drive on the right-hand side of the road.

Systems have become ingrained in our thinking. We unquestioningly, *even unthinkingly,* accept the requirement that you *must* play by the rules of the game. Only a lunatic would do otherwise. Right?

Where Systems Go Wrong

If systems bring us so much good, who, then, can fault these procedures that assure us an unparalleled standard of living?

I can. And so can millions of other Americans who have discovered that good systems can go bad and, when they do, they cry out to be Beaten with a capital B; to be circumvented, overcome, and defeated.

Interestingly enough, it is not the systems themselves that are to blame for the faults of U.S. enterprise. A system, after all, is just the methodology for doing something, not the something itself. Rather, the blame lies in the "glue" that holds systems together. That sticky stuff is *bureaucracy* and it has bollixed more good business systems than all other problems combined. Bureaucracy turns good systems into bad. Bureaucracy turns simple, useful programs and procedures into inflexible rules and regulations and the employees who work for them from creative, enterprising stem-winders into impersonal, unthinking troglodytes.

Whether we like it or not, we live cheek by jowl with bureaucratic systems of all kinds. And *dealing with* bureaucratic systems is nothing more than the flip side of *working for* a bureaucratic system. If you have a job, if you manage a company, you probably *work for* a business that's far too bureaucratic. And that means, *ipso facto,* the less freedom you have to flex your creative muscles and fully realize your potential.

What's a Bureaucratic System?

When we think of formal bureaucracies or "bureaumania" as I like to call them, we think of a system in which the means become ends in themselves and the greater good is often lost in the press for uniformity. Parochial or sectional interests are swapped for the good of the whole. And that means individuality, your individuality, is largely an anathema to the System.

Worst of all, bureaucratic systems left uncontrolled have a nasty habit of becoming increasingly entrenched, more bureaucratic, more corrupt, and perpetually more narrow-minded. They are more difficult to work with, just as they are more difficult to work *for.*

The Components of a Bureaucracy

The essence of the bureaucratic system—because it is a system—is a series of controls—rules, really—that are established to enlarge and perpetuate its own existence and the methodologies that enforce compliance. And whether the rules are oral or written, they are meant to rigidly define business operations.

The textbook definition of the bureaucratic organization suggests a system marked by:

- *Standardized procedures:* Pronounced rules exist, particularly those based on written documents like SOPs and employee manuals, and there are sanctions against challenging them.
- *Formalized divisions:* Grouping responsibility together with delimited authority and responsibilities. ("I can't do that. That's Brenda's job." Alternately, "That's not our department's job, it belongs to sales.")
- *Inside the box thinking:* Bureaucracies eschew creativity and reward behavior that doesn't "rock the boat" with continued employment. Accordingly, new, challenging ideas and opinions are clearly unrequited.
- *Hierarchical structure:* The typical Christmas tree-like organizational chart defining grades or ranks with respective responsibilities and matching coercive powers.
- *Impersonal relationships:* Both within and without the business or governmental unit, this is the one-size-fits-everybody approach to customer service. (It's like trying to order ham and eggs at the

Olympia Café in that old *Saturday Night Live* skit: "Cheeseburger, cheeseburger, cheeseburger . . . Pepsi, no Coke, no fries—chips.")

■ *Job placement dependent:* Technical qualifications and work rewarded according to a systematized formula reflecting job title and longevity. ("I can't get a raise because I have maxed out my grade level.")

What's wrong with these definitions? Well, nothing if you're brain dead. Bureaucratic systems do "git'er done." You do get your insurance policy. (Even if you are a cave man.) The bank doesn't (often) lose your last deposit. The IRS does make life miserable. Then, of course, there is the FEMA system, but the exception always does prove the rule.

But just as often these systems deliver a ponderously slow, unimaginative, impersonal brand of "one-size-fits-all" product or service. Their bureaucratic nature robs them of their real ability to generate true value for their employees and the changing tastes of the publics they serve. And since that is true for the customer of such a business, it is true for the employee as well who works in a nightmare environment where new ideas are so often stillborn.

Where would Apple be if Steve Jobs had been working for IBM? Where would Fred Smith be if he had entered the package delivery business thinking like the U.S. Postal Service? Where would Richard Branson be if he thought like United or Northwest Airlines? See what I mean?

How Bureaucratic Systems Create Problems

Bureaucracies, by their very nature, create their own problems. Often, the lines of authority and responsibility are so rigidly drawn that breakdowns and slowdowns occur. Any time you have the attitude that a particular competence is "out of your jurisdiction," prompt delivery of services will fall between the cracks.

Group thinking seeps into the organization and employees are unwilling to offer dissenting opinions even when such views are better founded than those held by the majority. (Which is, after all, always correct, isn't it?) Committees formed to solve problems unwittingly become instruments of stagnation where employees actually hide from true entrepreneurial decision-making responsibility. The inflexibility of processes and procedures render the corporate decision-making process burdensomely slow, and at times, frozen in indecision.

The bureaucratic system of rules can produce unwanted, even counterproductive consequences. Remember the book (and movie) *Catch-22*? The Joseph Heller work adroitly captures the absurdity of living by the rules of others, whether those rules are delivered by governments, corporate systems, families, or friends.

Catch-22, you'll recall, was the bureaucratic rule government imposed to validate the flying readiness of World War II bombardiers. The rule was neatly summed up by Heller as follows:

There was only one catch and that was Catch-22, which specified that a concern for one's safety in the face of dangers that were real and immediate was the process of a rational mind. [Capt.] Orr was crazy and could be grounded. All he had to do was ask; and as soon as he did, he would no longer be crazy and would have to fly more missions. Orr (Bob Balaban in the film) would be crazy to fly more missions and sane if he didn't, but if he was sane he had to fly them. If he flew them he was crazy and didn't have to; but if he didn't want to he was sane and had to. Yossarian (Alan Arkin) was moved very deeply by the absolute simplicity of this clause of Catch-22 and let out a respectful whistle. "That's some catch, that Catch-22," he observed. "It's the best there is," Doc Daneeka agreed.

—*Catch-22 by Joseph Heller*

Lest you think that such bizarre results happen only in movies, guess again. That kind of bureaucratic bumbling occurred when California judges applied that state's infamous "three-strikes-and-you're-out" law. Imagine some downtrodden fool drawing a life sentence for shoplifting some golf clubs while another was slapped with 25 years to life with no parole for swiping a slice of pepperoni pizza. Sad but true. Only later did the state pass new legislation to curb some, but by no means all, of the unintended effects of this Draconian law.

The reduction of modern corporate management to an inflexible system, a set of rules, is demeaning to all of us, but most of all to those of us who want to do better. If you are one of those people, you are the one I seek to reach because the glaring truth is that the more bureaucratic the environment in which you work, the more limited you'll be in your capacity to perform, contribute, and add value to the business. That means your financial success will be abridged accordingly and that affects the car you drive, the house you live in, the vacations you don't take. To adhere to such a program is a surefire way to inhibit the individuality that we all crave in the businesses we work for, and in the companies with whom we do business. And it's this individual treatment that's the first element to go in the system.

Maximilian Weber, the German political economist and self-professed guru of the bureaucratic way of life, wrote glowingly of bureaucracy in his essay, *The Protestant Ethic and the Spirit of Capitalism* (New York, NY: Routledge Education, Taylor & Francis Group, 2001). Although Weber never met a bureaucracy he didn't like, he pointed out in his work that bureaucracy starts falling apart when decisions are made on an *individual* basis—the very basis of the entrepreneurial freedom we need in an entrepreneurial culture.

The Real Cost of Bureaucracy

Bureaucratic systems can limit you, they tend to control your thoughts and eliminate innovation and creativity. What that should mean to you is this: Profitability suffers and everybody takes a financial hit—management, employees, shareholders, vendors, and customers. But employees take the biggest brunt since they seldom share in the very value they help to create.

Karl Marx noted that bureaucratic fallout when he said that bureaucracies rarely create new wealth by themselves. Instead, they control the production, distribution, and consumption of wealth and it's the employee who suffers most greatly:

> *The worker becomes all the poorer the more wealth he produces, the more his production increases in power and range. The worker becomes an ever cheaper commodity the more commodities he creates. With the* **increasing** *value of the world of things proceeds in direct proportion to the* **devaluation** *of the world of men. Labor produces not only commodities; it produces itself and the worker as a* **commodity**—*and does so in the proportion in which it produces commodities generally.*

—*Karl Marx,* Economic and Philosophic Manuscripts

Of course, it is not all about material things. It comes down to what we call "the quality of life." The bottom line is: If you want to chart new territory, create new ideas, new thinking, a new business, a new way of doing things so you can maximize your life's career contributions, you've got to beat the system that prevents you from doing so.

Is There Any Hope?

My experience and beliefs tell me there is more than hope—there is a real opportunity to beat the system. However, in order to do so, we need to understand and employ a few simple secrets. As strong as a bureaucracy is, it is a *fixed, inflexible* system. All fixed and inflexible systems, no matter how strong or entrenched they may appear to be, are susceptible to attack and defeat. Just ask the French about the Maginot line!

Bureaucratic systems are vulnerable when exposed to creativity, innovation, responsible risk taking, open communication, a consistent vision, and ethical leadership. Put all these together on the same team and you create a powerful force. This force is called an *entrepreneurial culture* and it is just what is needed to beat the system.

And that's what this book seeks to provide. I'm hoping it will light the way for those of you whose entrepreneurial juices are a quart low.

No, I am not going to teach you a new strategy for eclipsing the odds on a Las Vegas blackjack table or how to beat a DUI rap in your local court or find a loophole in the tax law that will allow you to claim an African warthog as a dependent (actually, there's already a book written that treats that subject). I'm talking about beating the system of bureaucratic encroachment that can paralyze your career, your business, and even your personal life. By learning how to beat this system, you'll earn for yourself an immeasurably more productive, enjoyable, and fulfilling career—not to mention the potential for increased financial success. Conversely, every day you continue to work in a bureaucratic environment, you are bereft of job satisfaction and, most important, your ability to control your future. And after all, isn't that what working is all about?

Business systems are everywhere around us. Some are good. Some are bad. But uniformly, when systems go bad, you're likely to find that bureaucracy is what is holding them together. Bureaucracies are the glue that holds unwelcome systems together. The bureaucracies of the world have devalued our jobs and our lives in many meaningful and different ways.

The way to beat these systems is to overcome the dictatorial control of bureaucracy, that glue that holds together the systems we love to hate. And the way to do that is to build an *entrepreneurial culture* in a bureaucratic world. You've got to have a personal lifestyle that is entrepreneurial, have a management style that encourages entrepreneurialism, and build an entrepreneurial culture, whether in a department or a small company or a large corporation. With an entrepreneurial culture, you can beat the system that is based on bureaucracy.

Most of us are not going to have the chance to start our own company. We are going to be working in an existing company, and our careers are going to be controlled by an existing company. Chances are that company will have all the earmarks of a bureaucratic organization. And because bureaucracy *creeps* into businesses, if it's not bureaucratic now, it could become so in the future.

I want to help you change that mind-numbing, career stultifying prognosis. I want to help you create a psychological thought process and a management style so that you can operate with more entrepreneurial *balance*—even in a bureaucratic world.

The bottom line is this: If you don't develop an entrepreneurial culture to *Beat the System,* you'll be bullied, and eventually buried by the system. And building an entrepreneurial culture, while sometimes difficult, can be readily achieved if you know how. That's what you'll discover in the remainder of this book, my 11 secrets to building an entrepreneurial culture in a bureaucratic world.

2

The 11 Simple Secrets

Being an entrepreneur is simply living a business life as it should be led.

Mention the word *entrepreneur* and most folks conjure up an image of a wild dreamer who goes into business by the seat of his pants and risks all to make some elusive pipe dream come true. Nothing could be further from the truth.

The word *entrepreneur* was gifted to us by the French (along with wine, mayonnaise, and arrogance). It comes from the French word *entreprendre*, which simply means to undertake or to set out on a new mission or venture. As you can see, nothing in that description harkens any visions of high-stakes gambling or wild-eyed schemes to turn a buck.

Sure, there are those over-the-top entrepreneurs who perpetuate that swashbuckling image. Guys like Sir Richard Branson exude the sort of swaggering, risk-taking conduct that the term entrepreneur usually evokes. Branson, of course, is the founder of Virgin Records and an eclectic stable of pubescent virgins: Virgin Atlantic Airways, Virgin Mobil, Virgin Blue, Virgin Cola, Virgin Express, Virgin America, and so on.

One minute Branson's risking millions of dollars founding a new company, and the next he's risking life and limb setting a world power-boat record or attempting a transglobal hot-air balloon flight. I can almost see Brad Pitt reprising the Branson role now.

Will the Real Entrepreneur Please Stand?

The image of the entrepreneur as a daring adventurer who recklessly gambles with his life and fortune is grossly inaccurate. Historically, we think of such luminaries as Henry Ford, Thomas Edison, and J. Pierpont Morgan as the epitome of the entrepreneur. More contemporary figures include Steve Jobs, the Apple entrepreneur; Bill Gates, the tycoon of computer operating systems; or Fred Smith, the founder of FedEx. These are the kind of entrepreneurs that management consultant and author Peter Drucker had in mind when he said "an entrepreneur always searches for change, responds to it, and exploits it as an opportunity" (*Innovation and Entrepreneurship, New York, NY*: Harper-Collins, 1993).

These business entrepreneurs and others like them had strong beliefs about a market opportunity and were willing to accept what others viewed as a high level of personal, professional, or financial risk to pursue that opportunity. They all understood that the real risk for a true entrepreneur is in not taking the risk of success because the true risk is in not risking. It would be a mistake to limit our concept of the entrepreneur to these business giants. The true entrepreneur is not defined by the size of the empire, but by the style of the emperor. By that I mean that you can be an entrepreneur by running a mailroom just as much as by starting a FedEx. An individual managing a computer department can be just as entrepreneurial as Bill Gates. The guy who owns a gas station can be just as much of an entrepreneur as the guy who started Ford Motors.

A true entrepreneur is not determined by the measure of his or her results, but by how those results were attained. Being an entrepreneur is more about attitude than aptitude. There have been some very talented business managers who failed because they failed the test of entrepreneurialism. (We call them bureaucrats.) Likewise, there have been some people with very little apparent talent who achieve remarkable success as entrepreneurs. (These types are usually abysmal failures in a bureaucratic world.)

Entrepreneurialism is a way of living life, not a way of managing life. The real entrepreneur has a certain spirit, an élan and an approach to issues that is just different. And that is the key. In a system that demands sameness, the entrepreneur is willing to be different. Only by being different can things be made better. That is the philosophy at the heart of being an entrepreneur.

Taking this approach, a more useful definition of an entrepreneur might be this: "An entrepreneur is an individual with the experience to recognize an opportunity, the inherent instinct to visualize its fulfillment, and the courage to reach for it. An entrepreneur is, by nature, a leader who has the talent to clearly, simply, consistently, and relentlessly communicate his vision to employees and to others; one who can motivate others to be successful because they believe it is in their own best interest to do so. And it is." Although I used the masculine tense in this definition, an entrepreneur can be male or female, young or old.

Using this definition, then, "an entrepreneurial culture consists of a group of individuals who have suppressed individual interests in an effort to achieve group success because group success will advance their individual interests."

These are pretty solid definitions but the devil is in the details—the actual practice of instituting an entrepreneurial culture in your job, your department, or your business. The good news is that entrepreneurs are made not born. The better news is that anyone with the right desire and commitment can achieve success as an entrepreneur. The secret to being a good entrepreneur lies in the simplicity of the concept. In reality, it is easier to be a successful entrepreneur than a bureaucrat. The entrepreneur acts with instinct and good common sense, while a bureaucrat has to know and follow the strict rules of the system.

The key to becoming an entrepreneur lies in the implementation of basic concepts and, as the title of this book suggests, there are only 11 simple secrets to learn to make it happen. But there is no need for you to carry out this task with the precision of a military field manual. The secrets are simple to learn, but don't let their simplicity fool you:

Secret 1:   Build parallel interests.
Secret 2:   Be an architect of the future.
Secret 3:   Be decisive, multifaceted, and ethical to a fault.
Secret 4:   Know the risk—measure the reward.
Secret 5:   Communication—be a shower not a teller.
Secret 6:   Power to the people.
Secret 7:   Become a trust builder.
Secret 8:   Sharing wealth increases wealth.
Secret 9:   Be constant, consistent, and concise.
Secret 10:   Treat important people like important people.
Secret 11:   Do simple things—simply do them.

Learning These Secrets

The important thing to remember in putting these 11 practical secrets to work in your life and in your business is to remember that together, they present a cohesive *philosophy* for being an entrepreneur. When I say philosophy, I mean that these secrets are a way to think and behave, and as such, it's extremely difficult to distill them into a series of steps the would-be entrepreneur can invoke like a some-assembly-required Christmas toy.

The reality is that these secrets do not stand alone. They are interdependent. It's not like you can accept five of the secrets and ignore the others. This really is an all-or-nothing proposition—a little like constructing a building. Each of the beams used in a building are strong and, in and of themselves, important. However, no single beam or even several are enough to support the building. They all need to be used and put in their right place. When in place, they support each of the other beams. Using the secrets to build an entrepreneurial culture is much the same.

As you move through the chapters, you will find that there is a good deal of overlap in these concepts, just as there is overlap in the concepts of honesty, trust, respect, and fairness. I encourage you to treat whatever repetitiveness you find as a bonus designed to increase your learning. I hope you'll learn a new way of entrepreneurial thinking because you are what you think.

Bureaucratic Organizations Are Not Born, They Are Made

A prerequisite to building or changing a business culture—whether entrepreneurial, bureaucratic, or somewhere in between—is a better understanding of the origins of corporate cultures. Having such a perspective makes it easier to understand the mentality of the bureaucracy, the difficulty involved in changing a corporate bureaucratic culture, and the most effective way to implement the 11 secrets necessary to achieve an entrepreneurial culture.

In this book (and everywhere else I am given a platform), I am quite tough on large, institutional bureaucracies. I am not apologetic about my comments because a bureaucracy, by its nature, often destroys or at the very least paralyzes, the value of the organization it infects. However, in fairness I have to point out that for a large organization to become bureaucratic, it must first experience the success of becoming a large organization.

Chances are that when these companies achieved their remarkable levels of success, they did so as the result of a unique spirit and culture that developed within the company. It is this distinctive spirit and culture that drove, fostered, and fed the achievement of success. However, this spirit of success is fragile and exists only as long as it is allowed to exist. To thrive, the élan for success must be nurtured and protected. If leaders of an organization fail to do that (as many have), not only will the spirit that drives the organization's success break down, but the soul of what the company was all about will be lost.

Successful companies start to die when they stop doing the things that made them successful in the first place. Successful businesses and the executives who run them become comfortable, lazy, complacent, and less tolerant of risk and less open to innovation. It becomes easier to allow rules to set the tone, rather than the leaders themselves. Such an environment is a breeding ground for the virus of bureaucracy. Such companies have forfeited the very culture that produced their initial success: Doing the right thing at the right time; doing it first, fast, and often.

In the Beginning

Business cultures are generally born with a shared set of attitudes, values, goals, and practices that characterize a business. These collective assumptions about how a given business is operated are gathered and stored among employees from the CEO down to the janitor and the mailroom neophyte.

Many businesses, but not all, begin their corporate lives with an entrepreneurial culture. Often, one or two daring individuals break away from the workaday mold and establish a new company. Because the enterprise is so small, they can manage it by themselves pretty much as they please and can make decisions promptly and efficiently. In the beginning, there are no rigid guidelines, rule books, bureaucratic hardware, or supporting paraphernalia. These individuals are very entrepreneurial in spirit—quick and nimble and often flying by the seat of their collective pants.

As soon as the company starts succeeding and growing, it invariably starts adding employees to handle the onslaught of new duties. After all, the owners can only wear so many hats. Into the entrepreneurial culture, then, come more formalized plans, programs, and procedures instituted to govern the behavior, responsibilities, and the jurisdictions of each added layer of the organization: sales, marketing, human resources, legal, accounting, and so on. Unless the leaders are very vigilant, it is at this critical juncture that the original vision of the entrepreneurs who began the business can become clouded and *isolated* from the actual employees who are doing the work.

Corporate Cultures as Organisms

Employees, like all individuals, tend to hold and repeat the behavior and thinking that has been successful in the past—good or bad. For example, cooking up corporate partnerships to hide debt might successfully create an earnings statement more palatable to shareholders, but as we know (and as Jeffrey Skilling can testify), it is probably not an ethical or legal way to achieve such a result.

When employees learn the behavior and thinking that works, they pass the information on to newer employees as part of their business socialization. We have a name for that: it's called *learning the ropes*. With repetition, these behaviors gain an enduring status until they become so embedded that few employees question the origin or even the suitability of them. They become as culturally institutionalized as employee manuals because there is often little disparity between what the manual says and what employees do.

How many times have you heard, "We do it this way because we've *always* done it this way," or "Our department doesn't do that. That has to be done by such and so department." Newcomers, of course, go along to get along and the successful behavior continues.

If a business condones backdating inventories to produce unearned tax savings, then repeated episodes perpetuate that culture of deceit. If executives accept backdated stock options for personal gain, the message flows throughout the organization. Likewise, good messages also stick. If organizational leaders have zero tolerance for anything that is not right, they produce a different (and I'd say healthier), corporate environment. But the point is, mental models of culture are (usually), unquestioningly accepted and perpetuated by most, if not all, employees. It takes time, but sooner or later, most employees learn the ropes, the ongoing culture, and behave according to what the system communicates.

Cultures Take Time to Formalize

The culture of most businesses today probably bears little resemblance to what their founding fathers may have had in mind. Who knows what Milton Hershey had on his cultural mind when he founded the candy company or what George D. Dayton was attempting to achieve when he established Dayton's Dry Goods, the forerunner of the Target Corporation?

It really makes no difference. Corporate cultures are often the result of years of collective group experience and, most certainly, they outlive their founders. They have been modified ad infinitum over time as newer management teams are hired to imbue the corporation with a culture that they believe to be the most appropriate. In turn, the elements of the business are passed on to employees, eventually becoming embedded in the latest incarnation of the business.

Carriers of Corporate Culture

These models of behavior and thinking are the internalized employee manuals that intuitively guide just about everything that happens in a given business. Here are just a few of the imperatives:

- What happens if I'm late to work? Leave early? Fail to show up at all?
- Does this company cut corners?
- How well does this company communicate its mission to employees? Rarely? Sometimes? Never? Do I even know where this business is headed?
- Will I be rewarded for extraordinary performance and if so, how?
- Is it permissible for me to be candid about the company's problems and opportunities? To offer new ideas and suggestions? If I open my mouth, will I be punished?
- Does the CEO say what he means and mean what he says?
- How fluid is job advancement? Are pay raises based on longevity or performance?
- Is *my job* viewed by management as important? Am *I* important?

- What happens if I make a mistake? Will I be fired?
- Does this company value my contributions?
- Is management accessible? Forthright? Candid?
- Is this a good company to work for?
- Can I try new jobs within the company or must I leave to refocus my career?

How we, as employees, answer questions like these and hundreds of others like them, determines the corporate culture. To change a corporate culture means that we must change the content of these corporate imperatives, and that's what the remainder of this book is about.

Spreading the Message

The corporate culture generally spreads from the top down using a variety of different methodologies, some written, some oral. The cultural legacy of any business is the framework against which all new thinking is compared.

Indoctrination of employees occurs on the individual level as employees socialize with each other by offering tips, tactics, and stories about their company culture, although they are seldom labeled as such. As employees, we learn how things get accomplished within the organization from others. We hear about what the body politic respects and what behaviors it frowns on. In short, as employees we socialize ourselves to be part of the business system—how to *fit in* to the corporation.

You, as a company newcomer, might ask a fellow employee whether it's okay to leave work 10 minutes early. She might answer your question with a lamentable tale about a former employee who got fired for doing just that.

If you volunteer for extra duty and get rewarded with nary a thank you for your effort, you're likely to share with others how you were treated by management.

Acceptance and Resistance

What's particularly important for you to remember here is that most employees—whether you or your fellows—accept and share values. If you do not share the values of the corporate culture, you leave and seek employment elsewhere because your values—whatever they may be—will be continually at odds with those of your coworkers. The bulk of employees who remain, however, not only accept and enhance the corporate culture, they seek out others with similar corporate philosophies to join them in the business.

At LifeUSA, for example, we rarely had to search for new employees because existing employees often sought out like-minded individuals to join our operation.

This environment may also cause problems. Because corporate culture values are internalized, employees react the same way to the same situations again and again. They don't even have to *think* about how to behave, how to treat customers, fellow workers, vendors, shareholders, and so on. Their behavior comes naturally.

That is both a blessing and a bane. It is a blessing in the sense that the corporate culture, once institutionalized, provides a nifty shorthand that helps employees easily decide how to behave and perform their duties. It simplifies the employees' problem of figuring out what to do in certain situations. It's simple. We do things the same way we've always done things because *it's easier to do it that way.* But, of course, the flip side of that paradigm is that institutionalized values might straightjacket creativity and a variety of other important attributes valuable to any business's continuing success.

Cultures Create Challenges

The problem with corporate cultures is the very socialization process that brings them into existence. Because it is the nature of business cultures to perpetuate doctrines of thinking and behavior, they can easily fall out of step with the real world—the blind will begin leading the blind. In other words, they can easily drift off into bureaucratic regimes. Just as surely as your metabolic rate declines when you get older, cultures tend—by their very nature—to become more bureaucratic over time. Keeping a company entrepreneurial in spirit is a fulltime job that requires continual vigilance.

For readers of my earlier book, *Cheat to Win,* you'll remember that I chronicled how the insurance industry perpetuated its bureaucratic structure and became completely unmindful that the industry staple—*whole life* policies—were a poor value for most policyholders. The industry had become ignorant of what was happening in the real world. That's what happens when a don't-rock-the-boat culture becomes fully entrenched. It ignores the real world, and all of the alarm bells that should alert corporate management to the need for change fall on ears deafened to new, creative ways of thinking.

I'm sure that in their early years, the founders of The Hartford, Prudential, and the rest of the big insurance companies, were probably a good deal more entrepreneurial in nature. But over time, bureaucracy *naturally* seeped into their corporate veins and they lost their souls. Corporate leaders clucked to themselves, "We're making good money. Why change what isn't broken?"

Why, indeed. Because in today's increasingly complex business environment, corporate cultures rarely keep pace with competitive reality and are unlikely to reflect reality at any given moment—*unless they're entrepreneurial.*

What Happens to Entrepreneurism?

The fact is that success and size often engender indifference. Many companies simply stop doing the things that they did to make them big and successful. They stop communicating effectively with employees. They start inventing more plans, procedures, and processes for getting things done. They take away the autonomy and the ability for people to make independent decisions and to make mistakes, because they are so afraid of losing what they've achieved. I see it every day. Their ability to make good, timely decisions is frozen. And even if they make a decision, they have to constantly control it.

A Case in Point

We are all familiar with the fantastic legacy of Steve Jobs who, in 1976 along with a couple of pals, founded Apple Computer as an entrepreneurial company that produced desktop computers. For years, the company did very well. But then it began struggling and the Apple board ousted Jobs as CEO.

Trouble is, the new CEO immediately implemented management controls, processes, procedures, and the company assumed that bureaucratic posture we all love to hate. In a word, Apple lost its core, its soul, and its spark of creativity. Ultimately, the company almost went bankrupt.

So what happened? Steve Jobs—the ultimate entrepreneur—returned to the company as CEO in 1997 by a desperate board of directors feeling the relentless pressure of unhappy shareholders. Keep in mind that Jobs became helmsman of the *same* company that employed the *same* people as his predecessor. Yet, Jobs rekindled that elusive entrepreneurial fire. The company regained its spirit and its soul. Its employees once again felt that they were contributing, participating members of an Apple *team*. Now Apple is one of the hottest companies around. And its stock has soared from an adjusted price of about four dollars a share to a multiple that might be higher than 25 times that when you read this book. Entrepreneurism as you can see, pays off big time.

The Story of AIG

Another example of the entrepreneurial culture at work is AIG Insurance. Under the leadership of Hank Greenberg, this business had an amazing entrepreneurial aura about it. It had a spirit that enabled it to become one of the most successful companies in the financial services industry. (I should offer a precautionary addendum: I may not agree with all of Greenberg's management style or some of his ethics, but when he managed this company it performed brilliantly, because he had beaten the system. He refused to allow himself or his company to be constrained by the bonds of bureaucracy.)

Greenberg recognized that the most important role of top management was to teach an organization, to prod an organization, and to motivate an organization to beat the system. If you don't provide that kind of leadership, employees, left to their own devices, simply follow the path of least resistance, which is to say, they follow the system. The challenge is that providing this kind of leadership is a difficult job because virtually the whole world is bogged down in a bureaucratic mindset.

From My Personal File

As I write this book, I am providing consultancy services to a giant corporation that has hired me to create a new, independent subsidiary to offer retirement income management services to baby boomers.

The company has repeatedly indicated a desire to create an independent *entrepreneurial* company. The trouble is that their leaders are ensconced in a highly bureaucratic corporation, which makes granting this kind of independence practically impossible, even though they give whole-hearted lip service to the idea of the entrepreneurial culture.

For now, remember that bureaucratic companies don't have the kind of soul that naturally springs from an entrepreneurial heart. When a company changes from concentrating on performance to concentrating on process and procedure, it loses the edge that made it successful. When you have managers who are more concerned about process and procedure than they are about performance and progress, the company loses its soul and becomes susceptible to bureaucracy. That's why Jack Welch, when he was CEO at GE, lamented, "What we are trying relentlessly to do is to get that small-company speed, that small-company soul, inside our company."

Protecting your business or your department from becoming bureaucratic gets more and more difficult the larger it becomes. With growth comes a sense of accomplishment that's often accompanied by an attitude of "we've made it." Sitting back and enjoying the success could allow the bureaucratic system to creep in, because maintaining the entrepreneurial culture requires consistent effort.

Changing a Bureaucratic Culture into an Entrepreneurial Culture

Earlier I mentioned that the cultural legacy of any business is the framework against which all new thinking is compared. Having said that, you can easily understand that introducing new behavior and thinking will necessarily be at odds with what we see through our rose-colored cultural filters. The very bureaucratic nature of organized culture opposes change.

This is, I believe, the reason why the American auto industry has experienced such precipitous decay. Steeped in the cultural success of their industry, the leaders were unable to react to a fundamental change in the nature of their business and their customers. Beset by the fuel crisis and then stiff competition from Europe and Japan, auto industry leaders may have *wanted* to make rapid changes in direction but a ship the size of General Motors or Ford has massive momentum (and desire) to keep moving in the same direction and, to everyone's peril, resist change.

Businesses are subject to Newton's first law of motion in the same way as any moving object. Sheer cultural momentum will likely keep the corporation moving in the same direction that it has always moved, unless a greater external force is exerted. Change may mean growth, but change also means risk and fear, moving from the known to the unknown.

Any time you ask yourself or your fellow employees to change, you're asking them to forsake attitudes *that work* under the existing regime. You're asking yourself and your employees to give up some of their past behaviors. In effect, you are actually asking them to start *thinking* again.

That scares many people in the same way that the introduction of a new computer system, or a new, speedier way of handling customer inquiries scares them. Humans naturally fear change. They often resent it and may even resist it. Your skills as a leader who can build a new consensus will be greatly tested.

It Can Be Done

This is not to say corporate cultures can't be changed. They can. Entrepreneurial cultures can be built from the ground up, instituted at all levels of business throughout all departments, and introduced to otherwise bureaucratic organizations.

First of all, businesses need to introduce new entrepreneurial models into the workplace because there is a correlation between organizational culture and organizational performance. And who's to do that? Well, more than one study has demonstrated that the most important generator of cultural change is the corporate CEO. He or she is the principle means through which culture is formed, disseminated, and accepted by an organization. As important as the CEO is in the entrepreneurial organizational struggle, I would argue that meaningful entrepreneurial cultures can be fostered by managers on all corporate levels, not just by CEOs. The IT department can be entrepreneurial if managed by an entrepreneurial leader. The same holds true for the public relations department, human resources, accounting, legal, and so on. What businesses need most of all are leaders on *all* levels who are strong enough to offer, support, and sustain these models.

Summary of the Secrets

The process of building an entrepreneurial business environment starts by first understanding that all business cultures are shared sets of attitudes, values, goals, and practices that characterize a business; and second, that these collective elements are gathered, stored, and used by employees who hold and repeat the behaviors and thinking that have been successful in the past.

Business employees indoctrinate newer employees by offering tips, tactics, and stories about their company culture, which is often codified in various employee manuals and guides.

Cultures of all types tend to perpetuate themselves, particularly bureaucratic cultures. Accordingly, bureaucratic cultures are resistant to change because they require employee participants to give up thinking and behavior that has worked in the past.

With knowledge and continual effort, however, all bureaucratic and supportive business cultures are amenable to change. The corporate CEO is the principle progenitor of such change, but managers and department heads on all levels can institute entrepreneurial regimes. And you can certainly do so if you're just starting your own entrepreneurial endeavor. The secret, as they say, is in knowing how.

3

Secret 1: Build Parallel Interests

Interests in parallel create. Interests in conflict destroy.

Remember the old Colombo television series starring Peter Falk? Each episode started by letting you view the crime and disclosing the killer. Then you watched the rest of the show to see how Colombo, the shabby, seemingly slow-witted LAPD lieutenant would adroitly work his way through the clues to solve the crime. It was an interesting way to hold the viewer, so I have decided to employ the same technique in this book.

Rather than starting with the simplest secrets (not that they all aren't easy to understand, yet challenging to implement) and building to an eye-popping climax at the end of the book, I decided to unload both barrels at the start and reveal the most important secret of all. (Besides, taking this approach could save you some time.) This is the one secret that separates the entrepreneur from the bureaucrat. If you read only this chapter, understand the concept, and make it the cornerstone of your philosophy, you will be prepared to do battle as an entrepreneur in a bureaucratic world—and win! In fact, this secret is so powerful that you wouldn't have to read the rest of the book because it is the linchpin of all the others. (Of course, you'll want to read the rest of the book, if only to see how all the other secrets work in parallel with this one.) Here is the secret:

In all you do, in all your personal and business relationships, seek to create and maintain parallel interests.

What are parallel interests? It is simple. A parallel interest exists when others care as much about your success as you do because they stand to gain personally from your success. A parallel interest exists when you care as much about the success of others as you do for your own success because their success assures your success.

If you as an individual understand, believe in, and employ the secret of parallel interests, you marshal a powerful force that causes groups to work together to support your individual goals because your success becomes their success. The employment of parallel interests is what separates the entrepreneur from the bureaucrat. Some form of parallel interests always exists within an entrepreneurial organization. It would be like a fish that could not swim; it would not be a fish. Rarely will you find the existence of parallel interests in a bureaucratic organization.

In today's highly competitive world—filled with well-educated employees and savvy consumers—the secret to achieving lasting success is a conscientious effort to avoid the traditional rules of leverage and conflicting interests and to replace them with the concept of parallel interests. There are many who may think this brand of selfless parallelism is a naive concept that is so ingenuous as to be believed only by third graders and the mentally challenged.

Proof Is Everywhere

The proof of the validity of parallel interests is everywhere. We live in an age where transparency in our dealings is everything. And the truth is, businesses cannot long remain out of parallel with any of their public before they are discovered and dishonored.

We need only look to Enron, Arthur Andersen, Bristol-Myers Squibb, CMS Energy, Duke Energy, WorldCom, ImClone, Tyco, Adelphia, Global Crossing, Merrill Lynch, AOL Time Warner, Health-South, and a host of others to prove the point. So prolific are corporate scandals that the average person now believes that good, honest companies are the exception, not the rule.

Bureaucrats resist parallel interests because they seem to embody all that the bureaucrats find threatening. Parallel interests appear to give up control—in reality they solidify control. Parallel interests appear to give up power—in reality they increase power. Parallel interests appear to reduce wealth—in reality they enhance wealth. Parallel interests create a true *power of the masses*. This is the reason why dictatorial governments and bureaucratic organizations work hard to suppress any hint of parallel interests.

Why, in the early twentieth century, did corporations fight so hard (including killing dissident workers) to keep employees from forming unions? Because they knew that if the workers were aligned in parallel, they would garner power to stand up against employee injustice. The workers were motivated to form unions because there were no parallel interests between the corporation and the employees. If the corporate leaders had employed the concept of parallel interests with the workers, there would have been no need for unions, and both parties would have been better off.

Parallel Spirit Within

If you think about it, having parallel interests is natural. Deep down inside all of us there lives in our core being, a spirit of honesty and mutual respect upon which all entrepreneurial businesses should be built—the principle of parallel interests.

Throughout all ages, we have understood and profitably used this fundamental law of nature—the power of parallel interests. Horses to a wagon or dogs to a sled are harnessed in parallel so their power can be fused into a single, dynamic force. A football team may have 11 individuals on the playing field, each with different talents and assignments, but the team is most successful if all 11 work in parallel to achieve a winning result.

For the same reason, we join clubs, fraternities, sororities, churches, and other organizations because there is strength in the unity of greater numbers bonded together in a common cause.

In short, despite strong personal egos, most of us desire to be accepted, to belong, and to feel we are part of something larger than ourselves. We are happiest and most productive when we associate with others who have interests we can relate to, interests that are *parallel* to our own. The true entrepreneur senses this drive and marshals it for the benefit of all.

This is true in business just as it is in our personal lives. Men and women in business desire to live and work in parallel. But in bureaucratic organizations where parallel interests are not present, the onerous pressures to perform, or to achieve profits, to amass material gain, can sometimes overwhelm and steer people to inferior goals designed to benefit the few, not the many. Recent newspaper headlines attest that far too few businesses practice parallel interests and as a result they are—often unknowingly—all the poorer for it.

Parallel Interest Business Model

The concept of parallel interests is not a business model based on the laws of reciprocal altruism. That is a practice in which one person provides a benefit to another simply because he or she expects future reciprocation. This kind of parallelism is *not* "you scratch my back and I will scratch yours."

Rather, it is a business model based on the laws of *common interests,* whereby individual participants who have a common goal benefit from working in parallel with one another—a synergy of mutual advantage. Win-win, if you prefer. The benefits from this association begin to flow the moment the parallel bond is formed.

This cooperation can arise out of the natural instinct of the participants, but more assuredly, it can be purposefully orchestrated by a leader skilled in what should be a fundamental entrepreneurial doctrine.

The principle can easily be applied whether you exert your leadership from the plush, corner office on the executive level or from the basement mailroom. And as you'll soon discover, there are solid reasons for applying this principle. Building in parallel not only makes you a more successful businessperson, it can make you a better *person.*

The key to its implementation, however, lies in its simplicity. There is no need for an encyclopedic tome with dozens of steps to be carried out with the precision of a military field manual. Achieving parallel interests is a process that is simple to learn. And to enjoy the riches it produces, you simply *must* do it.

Heart of Parallel Interests

The heart of an entrepreneurial culture built with parallel interests is a culture with the mutually advantageous compatibility of all business participants. There are some who confuse the concept of parallel interests with *equality* or an *egalitarian* society. That is not the case at all. Parallel interests create an *equitable* arrangement—fair but not equal—that is shared among all participants in the conduct of business: owners, management, employees, customers, vendors, and stakeholders of all types. This means that you—no matter your station in this community—can create a better, more successful place for yourself and for those you work with.

Here is an example of what I mean. When I left ITT Life to start LifeUSA, the idea of parallel interests was uppermost in the plans. This was accomplished in different ways with different groups, but let me give you one specific approach. LifeUSA was founded as an employee-owned company. Employees who joined the company became LifeUSA owners by agreeing to allocate 10 percent of their gross income to buy stock in LifeUSA. Employees were not *given* stock or stock options in LifeUSA. This was not an optional program. Those who came to work at LifeUSA were *required* to become owners *using their own money*. This put the employees in parallel with the founders of the company who also had purchased their stock.

The founders and the employees both had the same type of *skin in the game*. The amount of stock owned may not have been *equal*, but the manner in which it was acquired was *equitable*. Another important feature of this parallel interest was that everyone owned the same class of stock and no individual could benefit unless all benefited.

While I, as a founder of the company, may have owned more shares than others, they were the same class of stock purchased at the same price as everyone else. There was no way I could benefit from the value of the stock unless everyone else did as well. As a result of this parallel interest in ownership, a large group of people were working very hard to see the value of my stock increase because they knew that the more I gained, the more they gained as well.

There is one other important point regarding this type of parallel interest. The true entrepreneur is not worried about absolute control. We often hear of people who profess to share, but are unwilling to own less than 51 percent of the stock so they can maintain control. This kind of thinking is more typical of bureaucrats than of true entrepreneurs. Establishing parallel interests is not about giving up the leadership of an organization, but to be true to the concept it does mean that the leadership must be earned, not legislated by legal control.

As pure as sharing ownership is, it is not the only way to instill an organization with parallel interests. The concept of parallel interests is not pecuniary in nature. (But it does help when that is a part of it.) The essence of the concept is a group of people who are joined in a common effort for a common benefit.

Last Thoughts on the Core

In my first corporate job with State Mutual Life Insurance Company, my responsibility was to create a marketing program that would stimulate sales nationwide. The success of this initiative was important for the company and my career. At first, I was assigned an office in corporate row, called the "Core"—an area that was separated from the workers by walls of intimidation and moats of disdain.

Everyone in the company not good enough to be in the Core was assigned to cubicles in the outer areas of the company. It quickly became clear to me that my success was dependent on the people in my department working hard to complete and introduce the marketing plan. Yet, the accepted structure of the company meant that there was little to connect me with those in my department. The solution was simple. All it took was for me to move out of the Core and into a cubicle with the others in the department.

I am not sure how I stumbled on this approach in dealing with the people in the department, but to me it seemed simple, logical, and no big deal. However, two groups—the executives and the employees—thought my action was a big deal. Because no one had ever been moved out of the Core except kicking and screaming or on a gurney, the executives viewed my action as heresy and mocking the system. (How bright of them, since that is what I intended.) On the other hand, the employees viewed my action as a big deal because I had put my interests in parallel with their interests.

Moving out to work with the group on the project was viewed as a clear sign of respect for them and the value they contributed. I had picked them over the distant executives (who were not going to help me with the project anyway). Clearly, I had created a parallel interest with the workers. The success of the project became *our* success, not just mine. Those in the department were motivated to work for the success of the program, if only to show support for me and the action I had taken.

Remember, the objective of every business relationship is to get all parties in parallel; the business owners; its top, bottom, and middle managers; its rank-and-file employees; its customers; its vendors; and its stakeholders. The purpose of this liaison is clear: Your chances of winning are virtually assured when you make certain that the other parties win when you do. Winning, of course, means achieving the most successful outcome for *all participants,* including yourself.

Mac's Golden Rule of Business

To position yourself or your business to earn ultimate success, simply ask yourself: "Is this relationship in parallel?" By asking yourself this question, you can avoid the inherent inclination of outmoded business models that seek to win *at the expense of* others.

Accordingly, by aligning all business interests in parallel, the individual interests of many are powerfully directed toward the welfare of the whole. The result: Everyone benefits more abundantly; the rising tide of increased corporate success raises the boats of all oarsmen.

Unfortunately, this is not the prevailing attitude in business today. Too often, company management behaves as if the interests of the employees and other players in the conduct of business are at odds with the interests of the company.

Like selfish children in a preschool playroom, many business managers abhor the idea of sharing. They believe that anything they cede to other participants automatically means that less is left for them. So they hoard as much as they can—as much money, as much corporate knowledge, as much power, as much of *anything* that constitutes position, prestige, and wealth.

It is a hard lesson to learn, but it is at the heart of the secret to every entrepreneur's success: When you align parallel interests in both your personal and business dealings, you achieve power and success far greater than those who define relationships within the context of a power-and-control dynamic.

Why Work in Parallel?

There are a many reasons why you—both as an individual and a businessperson, should believe in creating parallel interests. However, none are as meaningful as these two: not only is it the *right* thing to do, it is also the most *profitable* thing to do.

"The path to financial and economic success," wrote psychologist Abraham Maslow, "is to treat working people as . . . human beings not only because of the Declaration of Independence and not only because of the Golden Rule and not only because of the Bible or religious precepts or anything like that, but also because this is the path to success of any kind whatsoever, including financial success" (*Maslow on Management,* Hoboken, NJ: John Wiley & Sons, 1998).

Difference between Parallel and Faux Parallel

Many companies like to lay claim to being in parallel with employees and others, but a closer examination shows that they are about as parallel with their employees as the Sunnis and Shiites in Iraq.

When *sharing value* is mentioned as core to establishing parallel interests, corporate executives proudly point to their "profit-sharing" plan. Let me be the first to say that *any* (well, almost any) type of profit-sharing plan is good. However, don't confuse most of these plans with parallel interests. There are usually two characteristics of these plans that make them much more bureaucratic than entrepreneurial. The first is that most of the sharing starts at the top and (maybe) trickles down. Even worse are the plans that only include certain qualified (usually the highest paid) workers in the plan. The significant weakness of these plans is that most employees allowed to participate either have no idea as to how the plan works or how they can have any direct impact on profits. As a result, most profit-sharing plans end up just like any other compensation plan in a bureaucracy. These plans favor the few and the well paid over the many and the under paid. In fact, such plans may actually create more bureaucratic conflict than parallel interests.

For any profit-sharing plan to be effective in establishing parallel interests, it must include all employees by starting from the bottom and working its way up, it must be based on the direct and measurable contribution of each employee, each employee must be able to understand the direct impact his or her efforts has on the performance of the company, and awards must be based on the individual contribution of each employee and not as a percentage of salary.

In reality, a profit-sharing plan should never be based on profits anyway. It should be based on the value added by *increasing* profits. Bureaucratic plans pay over and over for the same profits (remember, usually the highest paid are the beneficiaries) while entrepreneurial plans pay for new value added.

This approach may seem more complicated than the traditional profit-sharing plan, and it is. However, such a plan creates true parallel interests while the typical plan does not. Yes, it is sometimes more difficult to implement entrepreneurial concepts like parallel interests, but the price is cheap compared to the benefits. You could even argue that the typical profit-sharing plan—while easier to implement and pleasing to the bureaucrat—is, in the long run a waste of time and money because the results do not justify even minimal effort. Besides, implementing the appropriate profit-sharing plan that helps create an atmosphere of parallel interests is not all that difficult.

Taking Stock in Business

Stock option plans are another example of what some managers like to point to as an excellent example of creating shared value and parallel interests. Nice try, but no kewpie doll. That's because most of these programs talk the talk, but in the end the bureaucrats only pretend to walk the walk of the true entrepreneur. A closer examination of these plans exposes many of the same flaws as profit-sharing plans. For the most part, stock option plans favor the few and the already well paid. Rarely are options available to everyone in an organization. And, even if they were, stock options do not create a real sense of parallel interests across the organization.

For the power of parallel to be effective, those involved must believe that they not only have the power to impact the outcome of the plan, but that they will share equitably in the value created.

Creating Parallel Cause and Effect

True parallel interest concepts create an ownership, connection, and power right from the get-go. With stock option plans, there is little correlation between the value added and the value of the options—little cause and effect. By that I mean that there is very little to directly connect the employee with the actual work they do and the value they receive from the options. Most tell you that the real feeling of parallel interests comes with the feeling of ownership. Stock options tend to be viewed more as *incentive compensation* than true ownership.

Don't get me wrong, the idea of profit sharing, stock options, restricted stock grants, or any other form of corporate sharing is good. That is, provided the plans are equitable to all and not top heavy. Be careful about assuming that these plans create parallel interests because plans that clearly favor the few over the many can be even more destructive than having no plan at all.

How Much Will It Cost?

When I have met with business leaders and suggested they develop value-sharing plans that include everyone and work their way up from the bottom, the response is generally, "Well, that's a good idea, but it is too expensive to include everyone." Why is the plan okay for the highest paid executives, but too expensive for the guys in the mailroom? That attitude gives a clear signal that management believes only a few in the organization have the ability to add value; that the others don't count! Well, that's not parallel interest; rather it is a simple demonstration of conflicting interest.

If the plan is too expensive to implement for *everyone,* it is too expensive to implement for *anyone.* When a plan is structured to include everyone and encourages everyone to work hard for the success of the company, it will not be too expensive—it will be in parallel.

Remember, rewards do not need to be equal to create parallel interests, but they must equitable. It is okay for the CEO to make a million dollars, so long as the reward is equitable. For example, let's say the plan grants options equal to 10 times a person's salary, but beyond that all values are calculated and earned the same way. (CEO pay in relation to others in the company is an issue we won't address here, other than to point out that an overpaid CEO and an underpaid worker are not in parallel.) It is the plan that pays the CEO $1 million and the mailroom employee zero that creates conflicting interests. The bottom line is that any plan designed to *share value* is likely to be more in parallel when the plan is designed to build from the bottom—not the top.

It's about More Than Money

As mentioned earlier, creating parallel interests in an organization is not just about monetary rewards. It's also about mutual respect, something seldom found in bureaucratic organizations.

Let me give you an example of how a nonfinancial tool such as promotions, can be used to create parallel interests in an organization. In bureaucratic cultures, you generally find a look-out-for-myself-because-no-one-else-will mentality. This leads to the highly political nature of a bureaucratic culture (not to mention the distinct aroma of heavy brownnosing) where the interests of individuals are in conflict with both the company and many of their peers.

The true entrepreneur cares about his or her people, their success and their future. In a bureaucracy, the most important factor in filling a job opening (I'll ignore the politics) is experience. In an entrepreneurial organization, the most important factor is *potential*. The entrepreneur looks for someone with potential to grow into the job, puts him into the position (even if it is completely outside the previous experience of the person) and then helps him grow. If an employee believes that those above him in the organization (especially the immediate supervisor) are sincerely concerned about his future, then he is free to concentrate his efforts on doing a good job and making the boss look good. This is the ultimate in parallel interests and can be accomplished at any level.

Hiring from the Inside

There has always been a valid debate regarding elevating employees from within versus hiring experienced employees from the outside. Many say they recognize the value of promotion from within, but then add, "We just don't have the experience inside and must go outside." There is also the belief that it can be valuable to bring a different perspective into an organization because *inbreeding* can calcify the ability of the culture to respond to change and to grow.

My belief is that an organization is more entrepreneurial and in parallel with its workers if every effort is made to build from within. The bureaucratic (lazy) thing to do is hire experience from the outside. It may be more difficult and take extra effort to focus on growing from within, but the benefits of creating parallel interests with an individual's future is worth it. So-called inbreeding can be a problem, but one way to overcome this is by allowing individuals to move outside their comfort zones and take on new responsibilities.

There is another benefit for this type of parallel interest: recruiting and turnover. No corporate manager needs to be told how employee turnover can devastate net earnings. It is not unusual for some companies to have 10, 20, and even 30 percent annual turnover of employees. The loss of each employee can be valued at approximately 150 percent of his or her wage or salary because of reduced productivity, new employee training, and a host of other exorbitances, so you can begin to realize the enormity of the opportunity. It is no accident that organizations with an entrepreneurial culture founded on the basis of parallel interests have remarkably lower turnover rates than do bureaucratic organizations.

If an employee believes he works in an organization with parallel interests, there is little need or motivation to look elsewhere for opportunity. When the employee feels that his interests and his future are aligned with the success of the company, not only does he tend to stay put and concentrate on the job at hand, but he also becomes the company's best recruiting tool. In effect, the power of parallel interests is self-perpetuating. Employees are more than happy to bring in their friends, relatives, and even spouses to the team.

Creating Parallel Interests with Everyone

Implementing parallel interests in an organization is not just about employees. Following the philosophy of parallel interests can give you an advantage over bureaucratic competitors, especially when you include all stakeholders: employees, sales persons, customers, vendors, financial backers, and shareholders. Fostering a culture alive with true parallel interests marshals the inherent power of each distinct group to achieve a single purpose—the shared success of your business—because all participants prosper.

Aligning your organization in parallel with the interests of your customer offers tremendous advantages. Consumer surveys constantly report that most customers do not trust that companies have their best interests in mind. Rather, most consumers express a feeling of conflict with most of the companies they do business with. On the other hand, those customers who do feel the company respects their value as a customer and has their interests in parallel become loyal, long-term customers. Accordingly, they become the best advertising spokespersons a company can have.

A company out of parallel with its public soon suffers for its short-sightedness. If not at the hands of government regulators, then at the hands of its employees, and especially at the hands of its customers.

Customers need no legal action by government before they take their dollars and their business to companies where they are treated more fairly, to companies that offer products truly in line with their best interests.

"If a man can write a better book, preach a better sermon, or make a better mousetrap than his neighbor, though he builds his house in the woods, the world will make a beaten path to his door." This Emersonian logic can point the way to the power of parallel.

Developing Parallel Interests

While many companies fail to even make the effort, it is not too difficult to align the interests of the company with those of the customer. For example, in my business of life insurance when policies are sold, they are actually put on the books as a loss. It is not until several years later that the company can recover the investment made in new policies and start to return a profit. It is a true loss for a company to sell a policy today only to see it cancel in a couple of years. An insurance company only makes money on a policy when that policy stays active. In essence, the longer a policy stays active, the higher the profits for the company.

You would think that this situation would cause companies to design products that reward those who buy policies and keep them for a long time. You would think so, but you would be wrong. Even though life insurance products are long term in nature, many companies—in an effort to boost short-term sales—actually design products that reward short-term policyholders. This is done at the expense of both company profits and benefits for long-term policy-holders. It is an easier strategy—a bureaucratic strategy—but it is not in parallel. In fact, the interests of the customer and the company are in direct conflict, and it does not have to be that way.

A Self-Policing Environment

As effective as the system of creating parallel interests may seem, it is never perfect. Not everyone subscribes to the concept of parallel power. But when your corporate culture is in parallel, it automatically responds to employees who miss the message. Rarely will your management have to counsel or chide an employee for not putting in an honest day's work. The culture of employees in parallel naturally assumes that task, and frankly, they're much better at it than management.

Employees in parallel develop a self-policing or self-cleansing culture. Much as our bodies reject foreign tissues and organs, the body politic purges itself of counterproductive employees. Your employees adopt the attitude of, "I'm working hard to make this business more profitable for all of us. If you're not willing to do the same, you'd better find work elsewhere." When confronted with the company's *can-do* culture, complacent employees are encouraged to either participate or leave. Sadly, many of those employees who leave a company come to understand the intrinsic value of the parallel perspective only when they join companies without such a culture.

Why Parallel Power Goes Wrong

The concept of parallel interests is simple and straightforward. Yet, like many of the 11 secrets to building an entrepreneurial culture, it often defies easy implementation. This fundamental concept often becomes blurred, even expendable, in the light of human experience and teaching, and the process begins early.

Children, for example, are often encouraged at an early age to abandon their true moral compass and go along with the crowd. Instead of being special, just because they're different, they are pressured to see things the way their peer group does; to dress as they do, talk as they do, and worse, *think and act* as they do. And often, when children become adults in business, they may buckle under pressure and behave in remarkably similar ways.

In short, it is one thing to *know* what is right; it is quite another to *do* what is right. In the business world, a familiar phrase neatly encapsulates the resulting philosophy: "Everybody does it." Corporate leaders cook their books because everybody does it. They reward themselves with unconscionably large, backdated stock options for the same go-with-the-flow reasons.

Many businesses seek to take unfair advantage of their employees, treating them like cogs in a machine, rather than like the men and women who *run* the machine. Businesses drift out of parallel with their customers in their search for cost-saving economies.

We have been thoroughly socialized to view selfishness as a pragmatic concept to enrich ourselves. And if we do so at the expense of others, so what? The more money, power, prestige, and entitlements we have in business, the more successful we are. There is no need for us to concern ourselves with the lot of fellow workers, or those we do business with, or the welfare of the communities where we locate our businesses. They must fend for themselves. That seems to be the unwritten rule of business.

And yet, there is that still small voice within all of us that knows otherwise. The power of parallel interests is at the very core of the entrepreneurial lifestyle. Parallel interests become the miracle in business akin to the promises of loaves and fishes: the more you share with your fellows in business and in life, the more of everything that is created for everyone.

It is a miracle waiting to happen. It is a miracle waiting for you to make it happen—if you have the courage and grace to try.

Putting Parallel Interests to Work

Walk into any business where the concept of parallel interests is practiced and you instantly *feel* the difference. You'll sense that here is a different place to work or do business. You'll discover that your treatment, whether you are a customer or an employee, is truly the business of *everyone* involved. Everyone is working in parallel.

This spirit is as difficult to define as describing honesty, trust, fairness, or respect—even though each of these concepts and many more like them are at work.

The secret to making this formula work is not found by reciting a list of specific procedures. Success is achieved by actively, *sincerely,* looking for ways, as many ways as possible, to put your business (or your department or yourself) in parallel with other employees, customers, and stakeholders. A reminder here: *Your implementation mustn't end with the suggestions you find here.* They are offered only as guides to your thinking, to heighten your awareness of what is possible. Think of these offerings as teachers of fishing.

The honest way to put the power of parallel interests to work in your business is to begin viewing the world through the lens of others: other employees, other managers, other owners, other customers, and other vendors.

What that means is that you must break the common rule of business and exercise your role as a *leader* whose power arises not from coercion or domination, but from parallel interests. Real entrepreneurs—in any situation—are entrepreneurs because they are willing to sincerely put themselves in parallel with the people they work with. As opposed to the bureaucrat who takes action (if he takes action at all) to the disadvantage of others, the entrepreneur seeks to take action that is to the advantage of others, because that is his ultimate advantage. Consider this:

- The bureaucrat keeps others down—the entrepreneur allows others to reach the top.
- The bureaucrat hoards power—the entrepreneur shares power.
- The bureaucrat professes to know it all—the entrepreneur makes sure that others learn more.
- The bureaucrat stays isolated—the entrepreneur is accessible.
- The bureaucrat tells people what to do—the entrepreneur teaches people how to do it.
- The bureaucrat professes to have all the answers—the entrepreneur looks for answers from others.
- The bureaucrat takes all the credit—the entrepreneur gives the credit away.

Summary of the Secret

The greatest thing about being an entrepreneur in parallel with his or her universe (or almost anything in this world that is important) is the simplicity of the concept—like the simple ideas of being good or bad, to love or hate, to cry or laugh, to lie or tell the truth, to be in conflict or in parallel.

Fortunately, there is also an easy way to determine interests in conflict or in parallel. You know if you are being good or bad. You also know when you are doing something that is in conflict with the interests of others and when you are taking action in parallel.

In all of the entrepreneurial cultures I have been a part of, from the smallest insurance agency to the multibillion dollar corporation, I learned that the success of those organizations—the entrepreneurial spirit—boiled down to three simple questions:

1. What are the available alternatives?
2. What is the right thing to do?
3. Is what we are doing in parallel?

I have been fortunate enough to discover that asking these three questions provides enough power to lead any organization and that organization will be the pure essence of an entrepreneurial culture.

At the heart of being a successful entrepreneur is the sincere and passionate desire to be in parallel with those who have the power to impact your success. When an individual recognizes the success of others as the path to success, he has then taken the first—but most important—step to being a successful entrepreneur in a bureaucratic world.

4

Secret 2: Be an Architect of the Future

The entrepreneur is a human dream catcher who plucks the vapor of ideas from the future, gives them substance, and inspires others to bring them to life.

This idea that successful entrepreneurs are people who have mystical powers as visionaries of the future is an overworked cliché. No one has the power to see the future, but the successful entrepreneur does have the ability to recognize what the future *could be*.

Many people spend precious hours dreaming of the future they wish for, while the entrepreneur works in the present to make the future what it can be. Dreamers are wishers who see their dreams evaporate with the next lottery drawing or dead-end job. Entrepreneurs are doers who use experience, focus, commitment, and passion as tools to become dream catchers. The entrepreneur catches the dream and then allows others to live it with him or her. When an entrepreneur's dream becomes reality, it is the future.

The bureaucratic system is uncomfortable dealing with dream catchers because the system belligerently believes the future is supposed to be just like the past. The entrepreneurial dream catcher raises the specter of change along with an uncertain future and this troubles the bureaucrat.

Begin the Dream by Reminiscing about the Future

Dream catchers use a technique called *reminiscing about the future*. The good news is that anyone can master and use this technique. Because so few people actually learn dream catching, those who do can easily beat the system.

To reminisce about the future requires an ability to visualize the future *as if* it were the past. All of us reminisce about the past. We visualize significant previous life events—graduation, marriage, the birth of a child—with a vision that allows us to see the event and almost relive it. We can even tell others about it and take them with us back in time. The entrepreneur's ability to reminisce about the future is so strong that it allows him or her to take others back to the future.

Think for a moment, what it would be like to possess a form of intuitive reasoning that would enable us to reminisce about the future as easily as we do the past? If we could draw a picture in our mind of what we seek to achieve so clearly, so distinctly, that it shapes our present reality to the point where it actually begins to take on the characteristics of our vision. The truth is that when we use our power to live in the future as others live in the past, then the future becomes as present as the past for all to see. It can be followed almost as easily as any road map.

Bureaucrats argue that this is the sort of pie-in-the-sky fantasy practiced by the Harry Potters of the world. Their rules say that no one can possibly have the power to predict and actually influence the future.

In no way am I suggesting that entrepreneurs spend their time idly daydreaming about the future, but they do develop a concrete vision of what they *know* the future can be. They focus their actions on activities that transform that vision into reality. Simply put, although entrepreneurs know it is not possible to see the future, they do believe it is possible to take actions that allow them to shape it.

Certified Dream Catchers

There are many individuals who qualify as certified dream catchers; I offer two as examples. Interestingly, these men are not thought of as entrepreneurs, but are both science fiction writers. That may be appropriate because most bureaucrats believe the entrepreneur lives in a sort of fictional business world. And they might have a point because the really good science fiction writers often have their fiction turn into fact, just as the entrepreneur has his or her business fiction turn into business fact.

The two examples of individuals who learned to reminisce about the future are Jules Verne and H. G. Wells. Sure, these guys were writers not entrepreneurs (although each of them turned their writing into a very successful business and fought hard against bureaucracy). So what is it that these writers and modern entrepreneurs have in common when it comes to reminiscing about the future?

Well, first of all neither Jules Verne nor H. G. Wells ever attempted to *predict* the future. Although they took different paths in their writing, they both set out to encourage their readers to imagine what was possible in the future. Jules Verne was a student of engineering and mechanics. Even though rudimentary, submarines existed when he wrote *20,000 Leagues Under the Sea*. Verne came up with the idea of the nuclear powered *Nautilus* by pushing the extremes of existing engineering capabilities to the outer limits. (It is interesting to note that the dimensions and shape of today's nuclear submarines match almost perfectly with Verne's *Nautilus*.)

H. G. Wells was an avid student of what was then modern science. Using his knowledge of science, Wells was able to write about the "atomic bomb" (i.e., what he called it) more than 30 years before the Manhattan Project invented the first nuclear weapon.

So accurate were these and literally scores of other *predictions* made by Verne and Wells that they should be considered two of the greatest *visionaries* in world history. They did not predict the future; they simply visualized the potential of the future. They based their *visions* on information that was available to anyone. Like Verne and Wells, entrepreneurs are students of the current business environment and they use this knowledge to reminisce about what the future in business could be. The future does not just happen; it happens through the vision of the people who make the future. Jules Verne, H. G. Wells, and the successful entrepreneur all have one common trait: Using their knowledge and experience, they lay out a potential future and inspire others to make it a reality.

Entrepreneurs Make Reminiscing a Profitable Habit

Entrepreneurs and all successful people habitually reminisce about the future. They have a vision that, when combined with experience, they use to build their futures. Jack Nicklaus, arguably golf's greatest player, was once asked the secret to his remarkable success. "It's simple," he said. "When I stand over a shot, I visualize exactly what's going to happen. And then, I make it happen." Chris Evert, one of the world's greatest tennis players, is reputed to have once said, "I could see the ball hit the line *before* I hit it." Quarterbacks renowned for pulling out a victory in the last two minutes of a game—players like Joe Montana, John Elway, and Peyton Manning—have all expressed that same idea. They describe an ability to see the field opening up before the snap of the ball and they visualize the play unfolding.

George S. Patton (1885–1945) is remembered as one of the most successful fighting generals of all time. He seemed to have the uncanny ability to anticipate the actions of his foes. And it's no wonder. Patton was one of the great students of history. For years prior to World War II, he studied the battlefields of Europe and envisioned all the battles that had gone before and all that would come after. When queried about his success in battle, he said, "I see the battle before it happens. I've been there before." And of course, he had. He knew how to reminisce about the future.

Does Reminiscing Really Work?

Is it really possible to *reminisce about the future* or is this just some poppycock platitude someone dreamed up to sell success books? You certainly have a right to be skeptical, but my own personal experience and observations convince me that it is not only possible to reminisce about the future, but is a core secret of every entrepreneur who is successful.

Allow me to offer a personal example. If you had visited my office after I was made president of ITT Life, you would have seen a pyramid of 21 different business cards, all bearing the name Robert MacDonald, framed and hanging on the wall near my desk. Some who observed this carefully framed career history might have considered it as nothing more than an executive ego trip where the top dog has your attention and his wall hanging brags about his meteoric rise from rookie agent to company president. That wasn't my purpose at all. In fact, it wasn't directed toward visitors to my office; it was directed at me—as a living symbol of something decidedly more important.

A few years before founding the company LifeUSA, I wrote a book titled *Control Your Future*. This book ostensibly discussed theories for achieving personal success in the insurance industry. Years later, I was sitting in the office of the president of Transamerica discussing the success of LifeUSA. This guy headed up a large, established insurance company and seemed fascinated with the rapid growth of LifeUSA. During the discussion, he casually said, "Mac, the first time I read your book I took it for a simple discussion about the life insurance industry. The second time I read it, I could see that you had painted the exact picture of LifeUSA as it is today. How did you know 10 years ago what LifeUSA would be like today?"

Not even I realized it at the time, but the book about how it should be done and all those business cards had been saved because early in my career I had reminisced how it would be to one day become president of a company. That visualization was a guide, a road map for me to shape the future.

My intent in writing my first book (*Control Your Future*) was to *visualize* how a successful insurance company should operate. The book served the same purpose as a filmmaker's storyboard creating rich images (visions others could see and understand) of the future LifeUSA and the success the company would achieve. When this type of tool is in place, decisions become logical because they are measured against a *specific mental picture,* a blueprint, of the objective to be achieved. It is actually possible to work back from that vision to create the specific framework and activity that transforms the vision into reality. Forget the predictions about the future that never happen; reminisce about the future and *make* it happen.

There is another special benefit the entrepreneur gains from developing the ability to reminisce about the future—he or she does not have to deal with the stupid bureaucratic business plan process. (That would be a great segment to add to the "Stupid Pet Tricks" and "Stupid Human Tricks" on David Letterman's *Late Show*. It could be "Stupid Bureaucratic Business Plan Tricks.")

Bureaucrats controlling an organization are convinced that the only way to achieve goals is to put together a plethora of mindless business plans, a complicated pro forma, and other financial planning busywork.

Talk about waste and futility. How would you like to have the value of all the time and money wasted chasing the grandiose contortions laid out in five-year corporate business plans? Have you ever seen a plan even come close to achieving one of these *forecasts*? Of course not, because these plans, even though they follow the proper rules of bureaucratic management, attempt to predict the future when what is needed is the vision to *make* the future.

Successful entrepreneurs, whether they are the mailroom intern or the CEO, share at least one thing in common—they always carry an accurate vision of what they are trying to achieve. They know exactly how their personal vision of success looks and feels—they even know what it smells like. Without such vision, goals cannot be achieved. All the business plans and corporate busywork in the world can't save the bureaucrat's sorry behind. Here is a case in point.

Who's Got the Business Plan?

In 1987, we were negotiating with Transamerica Life Insurance Company to provide financing for the start up of LifeUSA. Over several months and scores of meetings, we were slowly moving forward in the proposed partnership. I met with everyone who would see me, including the chairman of the company. I desperately wanted to tell our story and elicit the support of Transamerica.

Finally, after the idea had been presented to Transamerica's board of directors, I received the call we had been waiting for. The board had approved the recommendation of management to support LifeUSA, but only on one condition. We had forgotten to submit a five-year business plan for the development of LifeUSA. This was hardly an accident. We didn't have a five-year business plan. However, it was clear that we would not receive funding from Transamerica until we translated our vision into a specific prediction of numbers. Our CFO promptly assembled a business plan, and we submitted it to Transamerica. Of course, we knew that set of numbers and the forecast would never see the light of day again, but the bureaucrats at Transamerica were happy.

Feed Me! Feed Me!

At least bureaucrats are consistent about some things. Today, 20 years after the founding of LifeUSA, I am leading the development of a new entrepreneurial-based company within the bureaucratic confines of Allianz SE—one of the world's largest financial organizations. While the vision of the plan was carefully and clearly laid out and approved by Allianz in Germany (see the memo in Appendix), we spent almost as much time handholding the bureaucracy at Allianz. It was as if we were the nerdish florist in the *Little Shop of Horrors* and Allianz was the plant monster with an insatiable hunger for business plans. (Here is an interesting side note: Usually, once the bureaucratic business plans have been submitted and passed up the line, there are more negative repercussions for changing the numbers than in failing to achieve them. This only compounds the inflexibility and inability of a bureaucracy to respond to changing conditions.)

Most Business Plans Are a Waste

Traditional business plans, no matter how meticulously developed and presented are, for the most part, a waste of time, money, and effort. The only value in most of these plans is to keep bureaucratic bean counters gainfully (I use the term loosely) employed. Don't get me wrong, sound plans have their place. It is important to have an educated guesstimation of sales, revenues, expenses, and income, but entrepreneurs recognize that these are nothing better than a guess. What entrepreneurs understand is that business plans are best used for budget planning and measuring the progress of a company, but should not be relied on as the basis for determining or predicting the future performance of a company.

At LifeUSA, our formula for developing business plans was very simple. First, if the plans occupied more than two pages, they were too long. Short and sweet was our motto. Each division or department would be asked to list 10 operational priorities for the upcoming year. From that list, they would then pick the five most important actions that needed to be taken. They would then indicate and *guarantee* which of those would be completed and implemented during the year. Once those priorities had been established, the leaders were then required to develop a plan for implementation and report the progress made on the plan each month. In effect, this process forced managers to reminisce about the year ahead of them. They were not asked to predict results in the form of numbers, but rather performance in the form of implementing their vision.

We learned that when we became proficient at reminiscing about the future of the company and were able to identify the actions and activities that would enable us to achieve the vision, then the activities necessary for success and the numbers fell neatly into place.

I want you to notice that I said "we." We were a *company* of entrepreneurs. All of our department heads learned to reminisce about the future. It's not rocket science. It's a way of thinking that anyone can learn and they become more successful when they do.

What reminiscing about the future is not—and should never be confused with—is forecasting, dreaming, or planning. Forecasting is an effort to predict what will happen in the future, like picking the winner of the Super Bowl three years from now or what the sales volume for a company will be five years from now. Dreaming is a naive hope for something to happen in the future—such as being happy, achieving riches, or success. Planning is compiling a list of specific actions to take in an effort to achieve a stated objective.

Reminiscing about the future encompasses none of these ideas. There is nothing soft or mystical (except for the idea of catching a dream) involved in reminiscing about the future. Reminiscing about the future is, in fact, a hard, serious, effective entrepreneurial management technique that is made more effective because the system for business planning has become so bureaucratic and time honored that few actually practice it.

To be a dream catcher, we use the sum power of our experiences, creativity, imagination, desire, and commitment to create a simple, specific, realistic mental image of what we seek to achieve. My visions of becoming the president of a company by age 40 and building a new life insurance company that could compete with the industry giants are both examples of reminiscing about the future. The key is to make sure the reminiscence is specific, attainable, and focused. Once the future has been visualized, then decisions regarding planning and forecasting are much easier and more realistic.

An Idea of Universal Appeal and Success

It is surprising that this technique is not used more often because the law of imagination is now recognized as a universal principle by those who study successful people. The images and ideas we hold in our minds tend to manifest the physical reality that corresponds with those images. A human being tends to act in accordance with the mental images of the future that he or she holds. "The imagination," according to motivational author Napoleon Hill, "is literally the workshop wherein are fashioned all plans created by man. The impulse, the desire, is given shape, form, and action through the aid of the imagination faculty of the mind" (*Think and Grow Rich,* New York: Fawcett Books, 1960).

In fact, this entrepreneurial talent to reminisce about the future has become so much in vogue that the current best seller—*The Secret*—is devoted to the philosophy behind the concept. *The Secret* (Rhoda Byrne, New York: Atria Books, 2006), does not use the term *reminisce about the future,* but the ideas in the book are replete with the philosophy. The contributors suggest that before we achieve something worthwhile, we must first have an image of it already alive in our thinking—our reminiscing. Once the image or the specific inspiration of the future has been created, then we have installed the guide for transforming the vision to reality. What's more, our brain has the power to do this automatically. When we reminisce, our brains automatically provide us with the specific actions necessary to make the vision a reality much like a guided missile seeks its target.

Perhaps Alexander Graham Bell summed up the entrepreneur's intrinsic belief in reminiscing about the future when he said, "What this power is I cannot say. All I know is that it exists."

There is another secret to the success of being a dream catcher by reminiscing about the future. A picture is of no value for anyone unless it is properly developed; especially for those who were not there when the picture was "snapped." When an entrepreneur catches a dream, it remains a dream unless it can be developed and properly framed. Once an entrepreneur has communicated his or her vision of what *can be,* in a form that others can also see and understand, he or she must frame it and put it on everyone's desk.

Once the entrepreneur has established and targeted a vision, there is no going back. Sure, the picture can be cropped to fit a frame, colors and hues may be adjusted, but the fundamental picture is never changed. What makes an entrepreneur an entrepreneur (as opposed to a bureaucrat) is the willingness to be flexible and to adjust to an environment that is always changing, when his or her picture of the future stays the same.

If you were to visit an entrepreneurial culture this year and come back a year from now, or three and even five years from now, you would find the members of the organization speaking the same language and looking at the same picture. Try the same exercise with a bureaucratic culture and you might see the same processes and procedures in place, but the picture will most likely have changed—probably several times.

For the entrepreneur there is one future. The paths to the future may have been adjusted, but not the future itself. And that is the real secret to the success of the entrepreneur.

Summary of the Secret

The fastest, surest way to become a successful entrepreneur and build an entrepreneurial culture is to learn to reminisce about the future. Through this simple, yet powerful strategy, you can visualize your future and then, working back to your present state of affairs, develop the plans and programs to make your vision come true. The principle works because, when you reminisce about the future, your mind automatically begins to produce the reality of your vision. And the more you concentrate on your vision, the more motivation and will-power you develop to achieve it.

Every person reading this book has access to powers that allow him to peer into his future. The entrepreneur does not believe that the future just happens. He believes the future can be created and made in the image he has seen. The entrepreneur knows that someone is going to make the future and sees no reason why he and those he inspires shouldn't be the ones to do it. You don't have to be famous or a special person to achieve the power to reminisce about the future, but you do have to think and act like a true entrepreneur.

The world is changing rapidly and dramatically. The business world, attitudes of consumers, employees, the government, and society are in a state of flux. Accordingly, the opportunity for a new brand of success is available in this country, but it's going to take a true entrepreneurial culture to recognize and take advantage of it. To be successful, entrepreneurs are willing to think and act differently than most. They do not allow themselves or those they work with to be constrained by the ideas and attitudes—*the rules*—imposed by bureaucrats. Like the novelist who is only successful when life is examined from more than one perspective, entrepreneurs recognize that success can never be achieved if the approach to a career or life, for that matter, is as one dimensional as that of the bureaucrat.

As the entrepreneur goes through life, there is one gauge he uses to measure the level of achievement. It is a simple question: Do I feel comfortable? If he finds the answer to be yes, then he knows that he and his organization are probably not following the true path to success. He accepts that any warm sense of comfort is generally the body temperature at the center of a bureaucracy. And—make no mistake—it is the bureaucracy that ultimately suffocates your dreams unless the system can be beaten.

The entrepreneur does not wait. He has the audacity to reach out and be a dream catcher. He flashes the boldness that allows him to create his own vision of exactly what can be possible. As someone once said, "Failure is the curse of complacency, but success is the child of audacity." Remember, those who dare, win!

The future belongs to those who get there first. By learning to reminisce about the future, you can be the one waiting there when the rest arrive.

5

Secret 3: Be Decisive, Multifaceted, and Ethical to a Fault

Entrepreneurs don't make decisions for their employees. They teach them how to make decisions for themselves.

Among the many misconceptions people have about what it takes to be an entrepreneur, are the beliefs that they are as decisive as dictators, as single-minded as lasers, and as ethical as politicians who think they won't get caught taking the money. For the true entrepreneur, the reality could not be further from the truth.

Some may be surprised by that statement because many assume the entrepreneur is the antithesis of the bureaucrat who can never make a decision. Others see the entrepreneur as being unable to multitask; being passionate and focused on only one thing—personal wealth. Most believe that, in pursuit of the ends, the entrepreneur will wink at ethics and use a sharp knife to cut corners.

As with most myths (except for Area 51 and Roswell), these attitudes evaporate in the clarifying glare of reality. Sure, there are entrepreneurs who rule so harshly they make Saddam Hussein seem like Mother Teresa. And yes, there are entrepreneurs who care more about making money than love. (Though not many of them!) And there are entrepreneurs who should be in the executive suite in San Quentin. Like most myths, there is an element of truth that perpetuates them, but the total picture is very different from the legend. To put the true entrepreneur under this cloak is like saying all those who drink wine are alcoholics.

On Being Decisive

True, the real entrepreneur is decisive, but that is more an adjective defining the personality, not a method of operation. There has been this picture of the overbearing, personality-challenged entrepreneur rapidly firing off commands and decisions in machine-gun style having little interaction with those who have to follow or implement the orders. But that is a myth perpetuated by those of the Donald Trump ilk.

Real entrepreneurs believe it is a failure of leadership and management when they are forced to make a decision. It's not that they can't make a decision or don't want to, it's that entrepreneurial cultures work best when those involved are empowered to make the decisions. Contrary to the entrepreneurial myth, it is the bureaucracy that narrows decision making to just a few. In true entrepreneurial cultures, the decision-making process and power is spread throughout the organization.

When employees came to me for a decision, my response was, "Whoa, wait a minute. Why should I make this decision? I hired you to make the decisions. If I have to make all the decisions, then I don't need you." They would then be asked to define the problem, lay out the alternatives, and make a recommendation. If they were not able to clearly define the problem, offer multiple options, and make a solid recommendation they were sent away until they could. It's amazing how people who are empowered to make their own intelligent decisions begin to do so; and just how much better they feel about themselves for not having to come to their manager to make decisions for them.

When entering a meeting to review a problem and develop a solution or plan of action, I feel it is a failure if, at the end of the meeting, I have to say, "Okay, this is what we are going to do." Entrepreneurs go into such meetings with a pretty strong (call it decisive) sense about what action should be taken. However, unlike the bureaucrat who is simply there to show his power and pass decrees, the entrepreneur uses the meeting to encourage the members of the group to own the final recommendation. It is even better if they believe the solution was their idea, even though the entrepreneur knew exactly what the decision would be at the beginning of the meeting. It is only at the end of such meetings, when no consensus has emerged, that the entrepreneur feels the failure of having to make the decision.

Is That Being Less Than Honest?

There are those who will suggest that this approach is inefficient and even dishonest. If the entrepreneur already knows what the answer is going to be, why waste the time pretending the group is making the decision? Isn't it disingenuous for the entrepreneur to lead people to believe they are making the decision when all along he knows what he wants? That is not the case in either situation. The secret to being a successful entrepreneur in a bureaucratic world is to encourage others to be involved in making decisions.

The true entrepreneur is decisive when it comes to knowing what he wants and working to achieve it, but that does not mean that he is dictatorial. Instead he uses the experience, ideas, and suggestions of others to challenge, test, and verify his assumptions. He adopts the attitude that if he can't convince the people he works with to buy into and own what he thinks should be done, then he needs to rethink his position. However, for this to work, those involved must believe they have the freedom to offer suggestions and to not feel threatened by the their boss's ideas.

It is the bureaucrat who attempts to be intimidating in these situations. The bureaucrat is intractable, while the entrepreneur is encouraging and flexible. Intimidation is a tool used by the weak, not the strong. The bureaucratic system uses intimidation and the fear of repercussions to inhibit decisiveness in individuals. Bureaucrats fear being open to the ideas of others because they view such openness as a weakness resulting in the loss of power. Besides, they argue, if you are decisive you could fail, and the punishment for failure is swift and catastrophic (like getting fired, for example).

In a culture that is free from such punishing repercussions and the fear of failure, almost anyone can be decisive. For example, if you were guaranteed that you would never get hurt, you'd be schussing down those mountains marked *tres difficile* on Mont Blanc in the French Alps. What prevents people from making that decision is their fear of wiping out big time.

Sure, processing ideas and recommendations under this entrepreneurial format can be messy, but the real world is messy. Bureaucrats need things clean, neat, and complicated (to show how smart they are).

It is the entrepreneur who thrives when things are dirty, messy, and simple. What all this means is that the true entrepreneur does not make all the decisions. In fact, the fewer decisions he makes, the more successful he will be as an entrepreneur.

So, if the entrepreneur is not decisive about making decisions, what is he decisive about? The entrepreneur is decisive about cutting through the clutter of events to expose the core of the issue—paving the way for easy decision making. But how does he do that? The entrepreneur learns to focus on the critical points of an issue, whereas the bureaucrat gives equal weight to all issues within a problem. The entrepreneur is attentive to the larger opportunities and risks of an issue and leaves the details to others. The bureaucrat looks only at the details and never sees the big picture.

A classic example of a bureaucrat looking at the details and losing the big picture occurred while we were putting together the structure of AIMS for Allianz SE (see Chapter 14). I argued that the best way to implement a true entrepreneurial culture was to allow employees to actually own stock in the company. Some bureaucrat in the Allianz tax department argued instead for a profit-sharing plan. His point (and he was right) was that the adoption of a profit-sharing plan would save Allianz almost $50 million in taxes over a 10-year period. Admittedly, this is not exactly pin money, but it did lose sight of the big picture. In response, I was decisive about the fact that it was the entrepreneurial concept of ownership that would encourage the building of value in excess of $600 million in 10 years.

The entrepreneur is decisive about *what* he wants the organization to accomplish, not *how* it is accomplished. The entrepreneur has the ability to quickly identify and define a situation and establish priorities. He has a keen decisive sense of urgency and an instinct for knowing what to do. Bolstered by this belief, the entrepreneur is decisive in his support and defense of the effort.

Cost of Failure

When all is said and done, the true entrepreneur has the fortitude to be decisive because he knows the biggest secret of all: The cost of failure is pitifully small when compared to the rewards for success. Let me repeat that: The cost of failure is so much less than the rewards for success. In fact, there are very few things that you would do when the punishment for failure is catastrophic.

Sure, if you take your life's savings and plank it down on Jive Commander to win in the fifth at Aqueduct, you're likely to earn a painful and enduring lesson. But if risks are *managed* properly, the upside is always more blessing than the downside is bane.

But the system doesn't want you to believe that. They want you to believe that if you step out, if you get outside the system, if you are *decisive,* then the risk is so catastrophic it will take you years to recover. You can easily see why the system controls what you are doing and why it engenders that horrific fear of losing a regular paycheck.

Entrepreneurs seem to have a better ability to be decisive because they recognize that failure is not the end of the world. In fact, motivational speakers are fond of inspiring their audiences with tales of the repeated failures of famous personages. Here's an example:

At the age of seven, a young boy and his family were forced out of their home, and the boy was forced to go to work. When the boy was nine, his mother passed away. He had a job as a store clerk, but lost it when he was twenty. The young man wanted to go to law school, but had no education and no money. He went into debt when he was twenty-three to become a partner in a small store. It was only three years later that his business partner died, and left him with a debt that took years for him to repay.

He dated a girl for four years and, at the age of twenty-eight, decided to ask her to marry him. She turned him down. Thirty-seven years into his life, he was elected to Congress . . . but only after failing his first attempt. Three of this man's sons died prematurely: one at age 4, another at age 11, and a third at age 18. At age forty-five, he ran for the Senate . . . and failed to be elected. He persisted at politics and ran for the vice-presidency at age forty-seven, and again lost. Finally, at the age of fifty-one, this man was elected president of the United States. His name was Abraham Lincoln.

That's the legacy of true entrepreneurs. They have a vision of their future. They are decisive in their outlook. And despite failures, they keep coming back because they learn from their failures and say, "So what? That wasn't so bad. Let's try it again."

Entrepreneurs Stay the Course

One of the greatest values gained from entrepreneurs being decisive is that it allows them to identify, communicate, and stay the course. Napoleon Hill in his seminal work on business and personal success, *Think and Grow Rich* (New York: Fawcell Books, 1960), believed this quality of persistence is most essential to entrepreneurial success. "Persistence is to the character of man as carbon is to steel." Forgetting for the moment the political incorrectness of omitting women in this equation, Hill points out that the majority of people meet with failure because of their lack of persistence. "Success," according to Eleanor Roosevelt "is endurance for one moment more."

One of the most frustrating traits of a bureaucratic organization or a bureaucratic leader is the inability to remain focused and consistent. Employees working for these organizations or leaders become discouraged by this flavor-of-the-month style of management.

The problem with bureaucracies and why they often fail is that employees don't know where they stand. They don't know where their company stands. The ground under them is constantly shifting like a seismic liquefaction. Very few things are worse for the morale of employees than to have no idea where management stands on central issues.

Certainly you have seen how quickly a boss loses the respect of his employees when he garners a reputation as one who follows the idea of the last person in his office. Employees quickly give up on a company that grandly announces a major effort that will *make the company*, only to have that effort quickly abandoned and replaced with another and another in swift succession. This is not a problem the employees face when dealing with an entrepreneur. Entrepreneurs are decisive in the sense that they stay the course until they achieve success. To make both a mental and physical commitment to a company or a leader, employees must have confidence that they can rely on the constancy and consistency of the mission. Only a decisive entrepreneur can really give that to them.

Two points need to be made regarding the entrepreneur's decisive commitment to a goal. It works even if the employees do not necessarily agree with the goal or believe it is what they would attempt. When a leader is trusted, employees will follow him and work hard to achieve success as long as the goal remains constant. Being a decisive leader does not mean being inflexible. An entrepreneur has the ability to change and react to different conditions. It is the bureaucracy that becomes rigid and inflexible. In bureaucracies, whatever initiative is in vogue must follow the business plan. If things go wrong, the entire plan is jettisoned. The entrepreneur is decisive regarding the overriding goal, but totally open to adjustments as the plan moves forward. Employees love this because they can rely on the *what,* while feeling empowered to implement the *how.*

Entrepreneurs Are Multifaceted

Here is a very simple secret that entrepreneurs use all the time to get the better of the bureaucracy: *They live in the future but act in the present.*

What does this mean?

Well to understand this secret, we have to knock down another myth about entrepreneurs. People believe that entrepreneurs are all about this *big vision thing,* and that they pay little attention to details. The image that some people have of an entrepreneur is an individual who is focused so intently on building a sleek race car that he forgets to add the steering wheel. What distinguishes the entrepreneur from the bureaucrat is his ability to keep *both* the big and little picture in perspective. It's not that the entrepreneur actually *handles* the details, but he is clearly aware of what details must be handled. The entrepreneur recognizes that the way to achieve long-term objectives is to concentrate on short-term activities.

If details are so important to achieving the big vision, why aren't bureaucrats more successful? After all, attention to detail is the badge of honor for bureaucrats. The difference is that the entrepreneur has the ability to see the details in perspective to the accomplishment of the overall goal, while the bureaucrat sees the details as an end in and of themselves. Entrepreneurs see a pile of bricks and visualize how they will all fit together to form the building. Bureaucrats think about how each brick is going to be laid.

Haven't I Seen this Battlefield Before?

A good example of this secret is the approach of General George S. Patton of World War II fame. Even though General Patton never owned a business, he acted like a true entrepreneur. He spent his entire career in the ultimate bureaucratic organization and fought it every step of the way, and while he lost many battles with the bureaucrats, he ultimately won the war.

General Patton is a good example of this secret because of his reputation as a swashbuckling wild man who was focused totally on the big picture: to kill as many Germans as quickly as possible. What most people missed about Patton was that he was extremely detail oriented. There is a hint of this aspect in Patton's management style in a scene in the movie *Patton* when the general gets out of his command car and directs traffic. Who knows if that actually happened, but the action portrayed fits his style. Patton's ability to live in the future and act in the present arose in the Battle of the Bulge. No one in the Command (bureaucracy) believed Patton could pivot his entire army 90 degrees and move it 180 miles in 24 hours to save stranded elements of the U.S. Army. But, that's exactly what he did. How? Patton had trained his army to do this exact maneuver. Patton's attention to detail allowed him to accomplish an enormous goal. This is the sign of a real entrepreneur.

Entrepreneurs can be successful living in the future and acting in the present because—despite the myth of single-mindedness—they have the ability to be multifaceted in their thoughts and actions. In fact, the entrepreneur who is not multifaceted is not an entrepreneur but a bureaucrat.

When you think of entrepreneur Thomas Edison, you're likely to draw a picture of an avuncular, white-haired gent toiling away in his messy lab for months and years before *he* invented the light bulb.

The fact is the wizard of Menlo Park had dozens of other scientific minds at work in his laboratory, and one of the reasons Edison was such a prolific inventor was because, as a multifaceted leader, he knew that one of those details included building a *team* of like-minded scientists and motivating them with his salesmanship and coaching ability. And that is another vital trait of successful entrepreneurs.

Entrepreneurs Build Consensus

By nature, a successful entrepreneur is a good leader because he has the ability to motivate other people to fulfill his vision. The entrepreneur recognizes the big picture but realizes he can't (and shouldn't) make all the decisions; so while he sets the agenda, he empowers others to make the decisions. Accordingly, he must be an expert at building consensus among these employees.

What is it that entrepreneurs view as consensus? Well, I would define it this way: *A consensus occurs when employees take the ideas of the entrepreneur, adopt them as their own, and implement them, believing that they are the ones who thought of them.*

I believe that only a leader with the ability to be multifaceted can build such a consensus. This means that the real entrepreneur is not a loner, but is constantly selling, teaching, and coaching as he builds a team. The entrepreneur plants the seeds of direction and decision, but allows others to tend the garden. The true entrepreneur does not solve all the problems that may arise, but is a solution facilitator. He or she makes it possible for employees to expand their competence and expertise to reflect their true value.

Boeing CEO James McNerney tells it in a splendid article in *Fortune* (October 30, 2006, p. 98):

> *What I do is figure out how to unlock [employees' growth and potential], because most people have that inside them. But they often get trapped in a bureaucratic environment where they've been beaten about the head and shoulders. That makes their job narrower and narrower, so they're no longer connected to the company's mission—they're a cog in some management's machine.*

There are a number of techniques for turning cogs into creators: questioning, probing, suggesting, and being flexible. I discuss these more thoroughly in a later chapter. For now, remember it's the entrepreneur's role to build a consensus while maintaining control of the agenda. Solutions to problems are facilitated when people are motivated to work together and empowered with the right to come to a consensus. (Of course, it helps when people find they have parallel interests in solving problems. See Chapter 3.)

This is what an entrepreneur does that a bureaucrat does not do. A bureaucrat belittles people. An entrepreneur emboldens people. Bureaucratic systems make people feel like a cog in the wheel, whereas the entrepreneur makes people feel like they *control* the wheel.

Another element of the entrepreneur's "multifacetitude" (that's not a word, but bureaucrats would love it) is the ability—and strong desire—to communicate. Yes, I know the entrepreneur is viewed as the consummate salesperson, but this context goes much beyond that. (Communication is such an important secret to the success of the entrepreneur over bureaucracy that it is discussed in detail in Chapter 7. However, it is important enough to he highlighted here as well.) In essence, the entrepreneur *communicates* and the bureaucrat *tells*. (Am I being paranoid to think that our schools use "show and tell" to teach bureaucracy at a very young age? Bureaucrats are famous for showing a plan and then telling people what to do about it.)

The meaning of communication is to explain and to create understanding. Entrepreneurs are experts in it. Entrepreneurs *inform,* bureaucrats *give information*. You could count the grains of sand on the beach before you could count the number of memos written by bureaucrats outlining processes and procedures. Another secret of the entrepreneur's communication philosophy is that it is open and free flowing—it becomes the lifeblood of an organization. On the other hand, bureaucrats hoard, control, filter, and censor information. The entrepreneur believes that to be successful, people *need to have* communication; the bureaucrat believes that information should be rationed on a *need to know* basis.

Entrepreneurs Are Ethical Leaders

You probably would not believe me if I told you that I have never met an entrepreneur who was not highly ethical. I can say that because, by my definition, one cannot be an entrepreneur unless he is totally ethical. Also bear in mind that there is more to ethics than not stealing money.

Gary Kelly, CEO of Southwest Airlines, said in an article in *Entrepreneur* magazine (December 2005), that ethical conduct is manifested in the way you treat others in all of your important relationships: customers, vendors, buyers, employees, and shareholders. "If you don't have honesty and integrity, you won't be able to develop effective relationships with any of those stakeholders."

Exceptional integrity is one quality rarely mentioned in discussions about entrepreneurs, but it is probably the most important attribute an entrepreneur can have in the battle to beat the system.

Of course, all executives and organizations claim to be highly ethical in their beliefs and behavior. In fact, many organizations—especially bureaucracies—go to great lengths to quantify and define ethical behavior.

For example, in writing this book, I ran across a two-year study written by Arthur Andersen's Ethics and Responsible Business Practices group. The purpose of the study was to identify and measure the effect that ethics/compliance management programs have on the ethical behavior of employees.

Imagine that. Here's Arthur Andersen, one of the big five U.S. accounting firms writing in 1999 about ethical standards when, just a few years later, the corporation was tainted with accusations of unethical conduct in the collapse of Enron.

Here's an interesting little secret about ethics in business. The more detailed an organization is in postulating the do's and don'ts of ethical practice, the more likely it is that the organization has challenges when it comes to ethics. Ethical behavior is not legislated, it is lived.

The most important determinant of organizational ethics is the leader. In a variety of ways, he makes known what he expects from himself and others in the organization. In upcoming chapters, we will find a great deal of communication about organizational values—whether entrepreneurial, bureaucratic, or something in between—among employees. Because the CEO is considered to be the chief progenitor of a company's system, employees learn from his spoken and unspoken actions.

If there's a guy in the corner office whose morals are a bit shady, don't be surprised if such behavior seeps into other levels. Pretty soon you've got a company packed with employees who behave like Enron energy traders whose crafty schemes artificially drove up electric prices and ripped off billions of dollars from Californians. Even though Ken Lay claimed a lack of knowledge about this type of unethical activity, he is the one who allowed an environment that fostered such activity. The traders were proud of themselves because that is what they thought they were *supposed* to do.

In businesses where honest and ethical behavior—in words and actions—emanate from the leader then the employees more easily resist the many unlawful or unethical temptations that are everywhere. The bottom line in this discussion is that the ethics of an organization should *always* be established, communicated, and enforced by the leader, not the lawyers, human resources people, or anyone else. The real entrepreneur understands this and makes it a priority.

However, there is even more to ethical behavior than not fostering bad environments. What could be more unethical than an organization that talks about (or even puts in writing) the value of its employees, and then, in practice, treats them as pawns. How unethical is it to talk of respecting employees and then be unwilling to communicate openly or honestly with them? What is more unethical than to put the interests of the organization in conflict with those of the employees? All too often we see bureaucratic organizations that judiciously adhere to the letter of the law, but totally ignore the spirit of true ethical behavior toward employees, customers, vendors, and even shareholders.

Summary of the Secret

The true entrepreneur exhibits strong core beliefs that are not compromised, qualified, or abandoned. Beliefs that include shared value, parallel interests, open and honest communication, along with the constant, equitable recognition of the value all stakeholders—employees, customers, and vendors—bring to an organization.

The entrepreneur understands that with true ethical behavior comes the needed trust that sets the table for the ultimate success of the organization. He knows that not only espousing, but living, this type of ethical behavior creates a strong sense of ownership among all members. It also engenders a feeling of participation for all, a common mission, and an environment that encourages risk and enables those who contribute to the company's success to share in the resulting rewards.

Those who seek the secrets to building an entrepreneurial culture in a bureaucratic world know that the best-kept secret about true entrepreneurs is their belief and commitment to fully ethical performance.

6

Secret 4: Know the Risk—Measure the Reward

Entrepreneurs are not risk takers; they are risk mitigators.

Risk is the 600-pound gorilla in the entrepreneurial equation. Risk permeates entrepreneurial issues like garlic in an Italian restaurant. Risk both discourages and encourages. Risk paralyzes many while empowering others. Risk uncovers cowards, heroes, fools, and fortune finders all at the same time. Some see risk as something akin to swimming with hungry sharks, while others challenge risk like a lion tamer in a cage. You can't have a discussion about being an entrepreneur without considering the impact and influence of risk.

Let me let you in on another secret: *Risk is overrated.*

The reason risk is overrated is because most people equate taking a risk with taking a gamble. The truth is that risk and gamble are antonyms not synonyms. By its nature, risk is something with an uncertain outcome that lends itself to measured management. A gamble has an unknown outcome and is impervious to external elements. In the context of an entrepreneurial discussion, it is important to differentiate between something that is *uncertain* and something that is *unknown*.

The key philosophical difference between the bureaucrat and the entrepreneur lies in the fact that the bureaucrat seeks only certainty, while the entrepreneur is willing to accept the uncertain. Interestingly enough, neither the bureaucrat nor the entrepreneur is willing to gamble in search of the unknown.

The entrepreneur is willing to accept the uncertain because he recognizes that while risks cannot be eliminated, they can be managed. He also understands that the reward for accepting the uncertain is significantly greater than the reward for being content with a certain outcome. Even more important, the entrepreneur has determined that the downside for failure in both the certain and uncertain efforts is about the same. In other words, the entrepreneur has figured out that the upside benefit for assuming the risk of uncertainty is significantly greater than the penalty for failure.

New Business Failures Are Abundant

Many people associate and interchange risk and gamble with being an entrepreneur because of the high number of business failures. Nearly 80 percent of all new businesses fail within 24 months, and up to 93 percent fail before five years have elapsed. But remember, you do not have to start a business to qualify as an entrepreneur; the vast majority of those failures happened because someone took a gamble rather than accepting a risk. Most of the businesses that failed were started by gamblers, not entrepreneurs.

Entrepreneurs are not gamblers, pinning the future hopes of their businesses and careers on the turn of a card or the roll of the dice. Instead, the entrepreneur is a risk *manager* who learns to manage risk by assiduously studying hazards to success and creating ways to minimize them as much as humanly possible. The person addicted to gambling, whether in Las Vegas casinos or taking on half-baked business ventures, always loses in the long run, and loses big. A person conditioned to clear, reasoned risk taking will win more times than he loses, and the wins will always be bigger than the losses.

When you understand what the risks are, you can find ways to help mitigate them. You'll discover that there is a good deal of risk in any entrepreneurial venture, but that is risk that you can control. Even if your company's success is based on pork-belly futures or the price of oil, there are steps you can take to reduce exposure and to soften the tide that may turn against your entrepreneurial efforts.

What Is Risk?

All too often when I address career seminars, I find that many men and women overrate risk. When I left ITT Life, my parents (bless their forever-caring souls) were among the many who asked me, "Why would you give up a good job and take the gamble of starting a totally new insurance business? Why would you take the risk of abandoning a steady paycheck and bet on the outcome of an unknown, as yet, nonexistent company, at a time when you are comfortably in your 40s?"

The answer is that *risks are relative.* In my thinking, the real risk would have been to continue working for a bureaucratic organization. That would have been a risk of a greater magnitude because I not only would have been unhappy, I also knew that I couldn't survive in that kind of environment and probably would have been fired. So the real gamble would have been to do nothing, suffer, and eventually get fired anyway, or take the *managed* risk and earn the matching rewards.

Besides, having spent over two decades in the life insurance industry moving from door-to-door salesman to company president, I was comfortable with my knowledge of the business. I knew the strengths and weaknesses of the industry and the competitors. I recognized an industry in the midst of fundamental change and developed a plan to convert the upheaval into opportunity.

While others looked on my exiting the cocoon of the bureaucratic establishment for a new venture as a pure gamble, my analysis convinced me that it would have been a gamble to stay put and a manageable risk to move forward. With one option, I had no control over my future (unless I wanted to give up and become a certified bureaucrat); the other option was a risk, but a risk I could influence. I realized that failure in either option would bring about the same penalty, while success in managing the risk would bring significant reward.

The Bureaucrat Plays It Safe

This is one of the big differences between an entrepreneur and a bureaucrat. The entrepreneur recognizes the risks involved in new ventures, but attempts to neutralize or eliminate them through good research and sound planning. These actions don't eliminate risk, but they help take the gamble out of what you are doing. Moreover, entrepreneurs have another related trait worth mentioning: They are convinced that they can command their own destinies; that the *locus of control* is within them. This belief becomes self-actuating and motivates entrepreneurs to succeed.

Bureaucrats, on the other hand, believe there is safety in doing nothing; that if you just go along and get along, ignoring problems and opportunities, you will achieve an *acceptable level* of success without rocking the boat or without ever suffering the pangs of failure. This year you're a G-13 earning $74,608, and two or three years from now you'll be a G-13 earning $76,802. It's as simple and as predictable as that.

In fact, in *Cheat to Win,* I mentioned a person with that attitude. He wasn't a G-13, he was a hard-working guy with several kids, and I called him into my office one day with what I thought would be good news: I wanted to promote him to director of agent training and give him a nice raise.

But surprise, surprise! The guy turned me down flat. He said, "Well I don't want to be visible, I just want to be where I am. Nobody sees me. I do my job. I am just happy doing that." The irony is that after I left the company, he got fired. He was laid off because nobody knew who he was or what he really did. He was so busy flying under the radar that he didn't even register as a blip to the decision makers. Accordingly, he was easily expendable.

André Gide, the French author and Nobel Prize winner, said it best (*The Fruits of the Earth* [Les Nourritures Terrestres, Book IV], Peter Pauper Press, Inc., Mount Vernon, NY: 1969):

What another would have done as well as you, do not do it. What another would have said as well as you, do not say it; written as well, do not write it. Be faithful to that which exists nowhere but in yourself— and thus make yourself indispensable.

What Gide is saying, and so am I, is that if you truly want to be free in this bureaucratic world, you ought to allow the vision in your heart to take flight, don't hide it under a bureaucratic bushel, and don't cower in the face of risk. The difference between bureaucracy and the entrepreneurial spirit is that the entrepreneur is willing to do something to create the potential for something to happen. Of course, the risk is that the entrepreneur may fail, but he is at least taking some actions, which gives him the opportunity to control the outcome.

The bureaucratic culture doesn't take those actions. It tries to prevent bad things from happening. Therefore, only one of two things can happen. Bad things will not happen or bad things will still happen and bureaucrats will fail. What the bureaucratic culture does not do is give itself the potential to be successful because by its very nature it is prevented from taking actions that enable it to be *successful.*

And if you're reading this book with one of those yellow markers in hand, mark this thought: if you are working in a culture that is more bureaucratic than entrepreneurial (which, I think, describes most businesses), you'll never know how productive, how successful, how affluent you *could have been* had you just allowed your spirit to run free in an entrepreneurial environment. Your talent, my friend, is a terrible thing to gamble with.

Rewards Always Outweigh Penalties

The bottom line for risk-taking behavior and what should be your guiding principle is this: the rewards for successful risk taking far outweigh the penalties for failure. Yes, there will always be those who want us to believe that if we fail when attempting an entrepreneurial risk, then all manner of curses and plagues will descend on us. But, that is just not true.

Before success comes to any entrepreneur, he is sure to meet temporary defeat and even some failures. The trouble for most wannabe entrepreneurs is that when defeat confronts them, they quit. That's exactly what the majority of men and women do when they answer to the term bureaucrat.

Would you rather fail trying or feel the failure of not trying?

Risk is one of the most overlooked areas in entrepreneurial businesses despite the fact that everyone knows that starting a new venture involves risk. Sure, taking risks and winning can be fun, just as BASE jumping and extreme skiing can be fun for some. But prudent entrepreneurs know the secret to success is taking care to minimize the risk.

It all boils down to the entrepreneur's experience and ability to manage the risk he faces. Every time a cardiologist performs heart surgery, there is a risk of failure. It is the doctor's knowledge, experience, and training that reduces the risk to acceptable levels.

If you think about it, the stated odds for the success or failure of a new business are meaningless. Sure 93 percent of all new businesses may fail, but that only tells the story of those who did not understand the difference between a risk and a gamble and as a result were not prepared to be successful. The secret is to figure out how to be one of those 7 percent who have learned how to mitigate risk and be prepared for success. You've probably heard the popular saying, "Fortune smiles on the prepared." Actually Louis Pasteur said, "Chance favors the prepared mind," but the point is the same. And that is, the true entrepreneur may not always win, but he does one thing that failures fail to do and that is to prepare for success. The person least surprised by an entrepreneur's success is the entrepreneur.

In ideal entrepreneurial situations, risk management is a fairly simple procedure including the following steps:

- Understand and be willing to accept the risk of being an entrepreneur.
- Identify a need not currently being met in the market.
- Create a solid, workable solution to an identified need.
- Enlist others who have a personal stake in your success and are willing to help achieve the goal.
- Make sure you can differentiate yourself from the competition.

Certainly success has been achieved without these ingredients in alignment, but when that happens, it falls more in the category of winning a lottery than managing a risk.

And remember this: Sloppy risk management can be worse than no plan at all because such an effort can give you a sense of security that you don't deserve. While there is always something unanticipated that can happen, preparing yourself to be in a position to manage risk will help you through many a bad moment. Risk management consists of identifying and analyzing the events that may cause loss and choosing the best way to deal with each of these potentials for loss.

Now, can this book make you a better risk manager? I hope so. Can it make you a proficient risk manager? I doubt it. But it has been my experience that the principle reason why many entrepreneurial visions don't live up to owners' expectations is because of the inability to understand the difference between a risk and a gamble.

Summary of the Secret

The true entrepreneur—be it someone starting a new company or reorganizing a department—is not a gambler or even a risk taker. He is one who eschews gambling (at least when it comes to business affairs) and attacks risk with the vengeance of a mongoose staring down a cobra until it has been beaten down to manageable levels. The entrepreneur does not move forward until the risk has been so mitigated by sound analysis and management that the potential and penalty for failure is insignificant compared to the potential for success and reward.

The bureaucrat sees risk and runs. The entrepreneur sees risk and tames it.

7

Secret 5: Communication— Be a Shower not a Teller

Effective, honest, and open communication is the lifeblood of an organization. When it flows freely, an organization becomes entrepreneurial. When communication is constricted, the organization atrophies into bureaucracy.

It is easy to spot an entrepreneur. He is the one who *always* wants to talk about his business. It gets to the point where people say, "Bob, can't you talk about anything other than your business?"

Entrepreneurs are this way because they are so passionate and committed to the task at hand, other topics of conversation pale by comparison. One thing you will never see is a bunch of bureaucrats standing around a punch bowl at a party talking passionately about their latest memo or new procedure.

But don't be confused, the passion for the effort at hand is not just an affliction of those who own a business. It applies to anyone with a true entrepreneurial spirit. At LifeUSA, employees (who at LifeUSA were also owners) would say to me, "Mac, working at LifeUSA has made me an outcast at family gatherings." When pressed for an explanation, they would say, "I have become so involved with LifeUSA that all I can do is tell everyone how wonderful it is to be an owner. My family thinks I have gone wacko because no one talks about his job the way I do mine."

Creating this type of reaction in employees is a powerful weapon that enables the entrepreneurial culture to beat the system. When working in an entrepreneurial environment, people cannot help but become passionately involved, committed, and concerned about the success of the group. However, rarely will you find employees in a bureaucratic atmosphere giving as much as one ounce of concern about the success of the group, aside from protecting their own jobs.

What you will likely hear is plenty of griping. Bitching about their predicament becomes an often-used escape mechanism for employees trapped in a bureaucratic culture, justifiably so. While a few get so worked up that they whack their fellow workers and managers (more than 40 people have been killed in U.S. workplace rage incidents in the past 10 years or so), discontent is as palpable at a bureaucratic company as esprit de corps is at an entrepreneurial one.

True communication is the secret sealant that builds and binds an entrepreneurial culture. There is no such thing as an entrepreneur who is not an excellent communicator. You will not find an entrepreneurial culture that is bereft of constant, clear, and honest communication through all levels. Show me an entrepreneur and I will show you an incarnation of Ronald Reagan as a *great communicator*. Few bureaucrats even *attempt* to communicate. Sure, they may talk about it and do a lot of telling (and yelling), but they rarely communicate. They don't convey the important information, the vision, the feeling of camaraderie that is so essential to entrepreneurial success. Show me a bureaucrat, and I will show you someone who views communication as unwelcome as visiting the proctologist (please, no letters).

What Employees Dislike Most about Bureaucracies

The number one complaint of employees working in a bureaucratic organization is that *they never know what is happening*. Want a litmus test for a bureaucratic organization? Just measure the output from the rumor mill. The more the rumors fly, the more bureaucratic the organization.

The rumor mill is a cottage industry in bureaucratic organizations because it thrives in an information vacuum. What creates this vacuum? The bureaucrat sucks up information and bags it like a vacuum because in the bureaucratic mind, information is equated with power and control. We've all heard the old saying, "Information is power!" The bureaucrat takes this quite literally, believing that if he has information that you do not have, then he is more important and powerful than you. The result is an obsession on the part of the bureaucrat to squirrel away information, which creates a (planned) disconnect with the employees. The entrepreneur also associates information with power but he attempts to use it to connect with members of the higher echelons.

The type of communication talent possessed by an entrepreneur does not require the skill of a dramatic orator. There is no requirement for an entrepreneur to be a spellbinder or table thumper. What is needed is an honest, deep-seated commitment to continuous communication and a recognition that there is a difference between showing and telling.

Communication Is the Key

Communication is a vital tool for the entrepreneur's efforts to express his vision of the future, enlist others in the effort, provide updates about progress, maintain specific focus on the objective, and reinforce the very concept of entrepreneurial spirit within an organization. (Whew, that's a mouthful!) The entrepreneur knows that when people *feel* involved in an organization they *become* involved.

The entrepreneur comprehends that for communication to be effective it must cycle throughout the organization—like our blood that constantly flows in and out of our hearts. If our blood did not circulate, we would die. When it comes to communication, the same is true for an organization. True communication is an all-encompassing process and not simply limited to passing on information. The entrepreneur does not seek to drown employees in information while starving them of knowledge.

Information that does not flow freely throughout an organization creates another negative dynamic. There's an actual syndrome (or at least there is now) called *power-man syndrome*. It occurs when a business leader is so isolated from unfiltered outside information that he or she never learns what is *really* going on. (Maybe we should call it the George W. Bush syndrome.) The problem in a bureaucracy is that when everything is learned from yes-people, nothing is really learned at all because no one is willing to tell the emperor he has no clothes. As a result, the leader—regardless of corporate level—inevitably begins to make almost unbelievably bad decisions and often destroys the enterprise he or she is trying to lead.

In his article, *The 7 Habits of Highly Effective Technology Leaders* (*Communications of the ACM,* vol. 50 , no. 3, March 2007, pp. 66–72), Stephen Andriole points out that "Communication is a continuous process. When things are relatively quiet, leaders still need to communicate what they are doing, the status of their projects, and their strategies. When things are bad, they can call upon a deep, continuous relationship with their partners and stakeholders to jointly solve problems; and when things are good, leaders can exploit their communications investments to make sure everyone understands the significance of the victory at hand."

Power of Intimidation

A major offshoot of the power-man syndrome is the element of intimidation. The bureaucrats controlling the system believe that the use of intimidation is a wonderful device that can be used to keep employees in line. How many employees in a bureaucracy are cowered by intimidation that causes them to fear *being out of step,* losing their jobs, or not getting the raises or promotions they deserve? Bureaucrats use the control of information to intimidate and make cowards of employees. The bureaucrat knows that an intimidated employee is a docile employee.

The entrepreneur recognizes that intimidation cripples the vitality of employees and significantly reduces their ability to add value. It is well established that intimidated employees are afraid to speak up and offer ideas or share concerns; they become wary of taking the initiative and, accordingly, their doubts become self-fulfilling. Individuals stuck in the quagmire of intimidation literally become drones, mindlessly carrying out a sort of genetic blueprint cloned by the bureaucracy. Of course, that makes the system all the more powerful and the bureaucrat all the more happy.

Good Communication Breeds Respect

Probably the most overlooked and undervalued use of communication is to demonstrate the respect the leader has for those in the organization.

Respect is the all-important bottom line of this secret. In fact, of all the secrets for building an entrepreneurial organization, none reaches so pointedly into the hearts and minds of employees than respect. Better than money, more sought after than position, rank, or perks is the employee's desire to be recognized and respected for his or her contribution to the corporate whole. That means employees desperately (yes, desperately), need to know that leadership is fair and honest and that they will be recognized for the value they add.

Not surprisingly, a lack of employee respect is the hallmark of the bureaucratic organization and, perhaps, of business in general. When denied respect, you can expect employees to *go through the motions* of working because they know that their ideas and their creativity will be mostly unrecognized. Why give the boss 100 percent, they reason, when he or she doesn't really respect their efforts?

Hallmarks of Respect

The essence of an entrepreneurial culture is the recognition of the importance, contribution, and value added by all members of the group. Effective communication weaves these important strands together into a fabric of employee self-esteem.

Bureaucrats and bureaucracies see information—both the hoarding and the controlled dissemination—as a tool to control the employee. The bureaucrat does not believe the employee has either the right or need to have any information other than what the system deems appropriate. The entrepreneur views information as a tool to recognize, reward, and inspire members of the group.

Some believe that communication is all about sending memos, posting on a website, having a meeting, or clicking off an e-mail, but real communication is much more than that. The power of communication is found as much in the intangible form as it is in hard copy and specific forms. This is where the entrepreneur shines brightly over the bureaucrat. The entrepreneur understands that body language, even his very presence, is a powerful form of communication. And the entrepreneur is a master at it.

Simple Acts of Respect

Just the simple act of dropping by someone's workstation is a form of communication. It is not talking about business plans, but it is a communication that you respect the person and they are important to you. Remembering a person's children and asking questions about them and being genuinely interested in the needs of the employee are powerful forms of communication. A bureaucrat doesn't do that, but an entrepreneur will make the effort.

At LifeUSA, I made it a practice the very first thing every day to walk around and stop at every workstation to greet each and every individual. (As the company grew, this became more difficult, taking over an hour by the time LifeUSA was acquired by Allianz.) This action was an easy, small form of communication, but it was very important. Even I didn't recognize the impact of this simple act until I missed a day or two and heard about it from people.

Communication is not just information conveyed; it is what entrepreneurs use to *bond* with the people they are working with. A bureaucrat uses the power of communication in an attempt to control people by limiting the information they get or by putting it in a certain way. The difference between entrepreneurs and bureaucrats can be clearly seen when you examine their very important and subtle uses of communication.

Be Open, Constant, and Consistent

For communication to build deep mutual respect within an organization, it must be open, constant, and consistent. Communication is not something an entrepreneur thinks about, it is something he lives. Communication for an entrepreneur is not a process or a procedure; it's as natural as opening the office each morning. Communication that is not constant and consistent is worse than no communication.

Start Early and Stay Strong

Earlier in the chapter, I mentioned that using communication as a demonstration of respect for all members of the group is mandatory if an entrepreneurial culture is to be built. People respect being respected.

This program of continuing communication to build respect started at LifeUSA the very first day an employee joined the company. I would make it a point to sit down with each new employee to thank him for joining LifeUSA and for *giving us something no other company had*—his talent. Again, it was a small thing, but it was impressive enough (I was hopeful) to demonstrate to the new employee that he was important enough to meet with the CEO on his very first day.

Another thing we did at LifeUSA was to have reserved parking spaces for all employees (owners). When employees pulled onto the parking ramp, they drove up to a parking space marked "Reserved for LifeUSA Owners Only." Bureaucratic organizations use perks as a way to communicate to everyone who is important and who is not. LifeUSA used perks to demonstrate that everyone was important. There were no perks granted to the executives that were not also granted to everyone.

As mentioned, one of the most important aspects of effective communication is the exchange of trust between the entrepreneurial leader and members of the group. Proper communication is a powerful trust builder. Entrepreneurs build trust with their followers by first showing trust in them. The way bureaucrats communicate—or don't communicate—demonstrates that they don't trust anyone, so no trust is returned.

Employees Deserve to Know What's Going On

Whether I was running an insurance agency, a marketing department, or a company, it was always my policy to make sure that any and all details about the organization—especially plans and performance—were consistently and openly communicated to all members of the group.

"Share the Wealth" was a regular quarterly meeting at LifeUSA. All LifeUSA employees were invited to attend the meeting when the results of the quarter were reported and dissected. Nothing was held back and employees were encouraged to ask questions. (The same type of meeting was held at ITT Life, even though the employees were not owners and our parent company, the very bureaucratic Hartford Insurance, hated that we held such meetings.)

There were many reasons for holding these meetings, but the primary motivation was to use communication to build trust and respect between and among members of the group. We wanted to convey the spirit, "We're all in this together, and you have a right to know what we're doing and how we're doing."

One other technique we used was to schedule what were called "Brunch with Bob" meetings. Once or twice a month, on a rotating basis, 15 to 20 employees were invited to meet with me in the boardroom for a freewheeling bag lunch. At these meetings (with no other management present), I would report to the employees as if I were actually making a presentation to the board of directors. No charts, graphs, or power point, just discussion. We talked about current plans, objectives, problems, and results. Those present were urged to ask any and all questions. Again, from my perspective, the primary objective of these meetings was to communicate the trust and respect that I (and all of management) had in the employees. If we had not trusted and respected these people, we would never have held such meetings. The bottom line was: Employees recognized this trust and returned it in kind.

Does This Communication Stuff Work?

Did these communication programs work? Well, from a performance standpoint, you could never convince me that LifeUSA would have grown from a start-up company to one worth over $500 million in just 12 years if we had not made the effort to have this type of communication.

The ultimate validation of this effort to have real communication throughout the organization came the day we announced that Allianz had purchased LifeUSA. Clearly, this was a surprise to all employees (as a public company, we could not disclose the discussions with Allianz), but when the meeting concluded, a number of employees came up to me and said, "Mac, we don't know what is going to happen, and we are nervous, but we trust you and know everything will be okay." That was probably the highest compliment I have ever received.

Even though I have offered only a few examples of entrepreneurial communication, I can imagine that you might be concerned about how much time this kind of communication took. True, this approach does demand time and commitment, but the rewards are more than worth the effort. That's what open and free-flowing communication is all about.

Treating Employees Respectfully Pays Off

Treating employees with respect and dignity is critical to retaining good workers, especially in a better job market. According to a survey conducted by Sirota Survey Intelligence and the authors of *The Enthusiastic Employee* (Philadelphia: Wharton School Publishing, 2005), employees who feel they are not treated with respect by their employers are three times more likely to leave their jobs within two years than those who feel they are treated respectfully.

The bottom line is: If developing respect is not an important part of the management philosophy, a majority of employees in whom you have invested time and money to train will walk out the door after a couple of years. This may be just a blip on the bureaucratic human resources longevity chart, but the company has wasted all that time and money only to have to turn around and find, hire, and train new employees. In the meantime, company productivity lags because the employees who continue to put in their eight hours daily may have mentally quit, and their performance will show it.

How well respected employees feel is also directly related to how enthusiastic they are about their jobs. Enthusiasm can make every aspect of your business more of a glowing success. As CEO of LifeUSA, many of our employees were very outspoken in their personal assessment of the company and its treatment of employees. In their phone calls, memos, personal conversations, and letters, they would frequently mention how proud they felt to be working for an organization that respected their accomplishments and treated them with the respect they deserved. This type of adulation is not important for the individual manager, but it is important for the overall

success of the culture and is earned by a management with communication of respect that is consistent, concise, and constant.

Trickle-Down Effect of Respect

One of the surprising results of the Sirota survey—and one that sup-
ports the employee-as-major-asset theme of this chapter—is what I call
the *trickle-down effect* noted in many businesses. The company executives
at the top get the lion's share of everything nifty a corporation has to
offer, and the rank employees get the scraps—including respect.

Employees in bureaucratic cultures feel that nonmanagement
employees are treated with less respect than management (especially
senior management). In fact, one recent study (*Two Ways to Improve
Employee Retention and Engagement: Treating Workers with Respect &
Dealing with Poor Performance,* Sirota Survey Intelligence, July 24, 2006)
showed that while almost half of senior-level managers feel they are
shown a great deal of respect, just one-quarter of supervisors and only
20 percent of nonmanagement employees feel the same way. It does
not surprise me to learn that the survey discovered that one out of
every seven nonmanagement employees actually feels he or she is
treated poorly or very poorly. Are you surprised? You shouldn't be.
Most bureaucratic cultures treat their lower-ranking employees like
cogs in an unfeeling machine, while top managers hog most of the
salaries, bonuses, stock options, perks, and favorable treatment. Nothing is in parallel. Everything favors top management.

Communication Is a Two-Way Street

Entrepreneurs know that if they talk with employees and get a real feel
for where they're coming from, they are going to be able to be much

more open with them, which sends a much clearer signal to employees about whether they are in an entrepreneurial environment.

Ask simple questions: What kind of communication do you get? What is the general morale and attitude of the company here? What is the best part of the company? What is the worst part of the company? It is amazing how people will open up to you about the company. The key is not the impression you get from the top, the key is to find people within the system to see what they say and what their attitudes toward the system are.

This may strike you as treading on dangerous ground. And in a sense, it is. You might get unusually frank and candid feedback. You may hear things you don't want to hear. But that's just the kind of feedback smart entrepreneurs need and want. They want to know how they're doing and how to improve the business. And even if employee perceptions are not totally valid, what is valid is that they *have* these perceptions, and that, in itself, is cause for future action by the entrepreneur.

With increased awareness, agreement about company goals, and improved communication of results, management can make quick and effective adjustments during the month. Everyone can remain focused on the ultimate goal, which is always assumed but sometimes lost during daily activities—making money!

Learning to Respect

Now, am I going to give you a laundry list of how-tos to earn employee respect? No. For employee respect to work—to pay dividends—it has to come straight from the heart. You cannot fake respect. You have to proactively seek ways to bestow respect on employees.

I know that sounds a bit sappy perhaps, but it's true. You actually have to *believe* that employees are your business's greatest asset, otherwise you'll only begrudgingly accept your responsibility to communicate with and treat them respectfully.

However, having made that point, I can at least provide some clues—a road map—for you to follow:

- Pay attention to your employees and show an interest in their development.
- Give employees the big picture. As I point out elsewhere, employees need to know the mission and goals of your business, and you must communicate to them how they fit into and can contribute to them both. They truly want to contribute in a positive way to the organization's goals.
- Encourage employee innovation and ideas for improving how your business is run. And above all, reward them for their efforts and do not punish their failures.
- Hold all employees accountable. One of the quickest ways to puncture the morale of employees and their willingness to give outstanding performance is when you allow slackers to slack. After all, who wants to give 110 percent when a colleague is offering only 65 percent?
- Pitch in yourself. When business is particularly demanding, smart managers and supervisors will ignore rigid employee stratification and climb into the trenches with their staff to get the job done.
- Recognize employees for their accomplishments, and provide them with the freedom to use their own judgment.
- Solicit, listen to, and act on work-related ideas from employees, such as input on how to get the work done.
- Provide employees with helpful feedback and coaching on how to perform more effectively.
- Value people as individuals, and give them a sense of being included.

- Encourage full expression of ideas without fear of negative consequences.
- Listen to and handle fairly all employee complaints.

Employees, after all, want the same thing *you* want.

Putting Your Plan into Action

As you can see, it's easy to develop a list of ways to show employees the respect they deserve and most of them don't involve throwing money at them. It's simple to do, and as I frequently say, simply *do it*.

Let me give you one example. At LifeUSA, we dreamed up a program called "Pride Awards" to recognize the achievements of our employees. We created a variety of pride awards built around the nuances of the insurance business. For example, we had an owner of the month (if you remember, all of our employees *were* owners because they actually owned shares of the company), a team of the month, and a department of the month.

All of these awards were presented at the monthly "Share the Wealth" meetings in front of the entire company.

At the end of each year, we had a pride dinner and ceremony during which we would name the "owners cabinet," the owner of the year, the department of the year, the team of the year, and the division of the year. These employees got prizes. They got recognition.

The important thing here was not the plaque, trophy, or bonus— although you can consider any one or all of these things. What was important was to receive the honor of being named, to have one's achievements acknowledged by management, and seconded by co-workers. Even those who didn't get named felt that they were participating and sharing because we had taken the time to acknowledge their work. It had a tremendous impact on people.

That was a big deal for them. And it was an even a bigger deal, believe it or not, for the success of the company.

Anniversaries Are Recognized

Another example of action taken to build recognition and respect was a formal acknowledgment of employee anniversaries with the company. Everyone who had an anniversary got recognized, either with a phone call or a letter from me. They were also recognized in meetings, but employees who were celebrating benchmark anniversaries (5 year, 10 year, 15 year, and 20 year), were invited to a monthly lunch with me and other members of senior management. We would go to a local country club, have lunch, and talk.

As CEO of the corporation, my presence was specifically included to send a message to employees. It said, "I am here today because *you* are so important to this company. You have given 5, 10, or 15 years of your life to this company, and I want you to understand that we appreciate that; we recognize that fact, and we want you to know that you are important to us. If you weren't important, I wouldn't be here today. Others wouldn't be here today."

But when you not only say that, but you *do things* to say that employees are important, it makes a tremendous impact.

Look at it this way, if Warren Buffett was in town and he was a big shareholder of your company, you would have lunch with him, right? Why, because he is important. So when I, as the corporate CEO have lunch with you because you have had your 10-year anniversary (instead of just sending you a plaque or putting your name in the house newsletter), it takes on a whole new meaning. I am telling you that you are important. That is what entrepreneurial cultures do. And to the employee it speaks volumes about how management views employees: "You are appreciated. You are respected."

But the employees respond even more impressively. They say to themselves, and in their every word and deed: I am going to continue to do the things that will get me appreciation and respect. *Your employees will work even harder.* Not because you ask them to do so, but because they want to contribute as much as they can.

If someone toils and toils and works hard, but doesn't get respect or recognition, what is their attitude? They say, "Why the hell am I doing this. Nobody cares, why should I even try this?" That is the difference between the bureaucratic culture and an entrepreneurial culture.

Summary of the Secret

When you adopt Secret 5 for entrepreneurial success, you open the lines of communication and create a respectful, transparent society where people are comfortable coming to you with whatever is important to them. Communications open up, new ideas proliferate, and employees are willing to step up with their best effort when mutual trust and respect are created.

The secret to being an entrepreneur is to be a master communicator. The entrepreneurial communicator builds alliances; never stops seeing the vision; makes decisions, but creates consensus, plants seeds, and stimulates solutions.

Real communication by the entrepreneur provides everyone with a clear sense of purpose and the urgency to achieve it. And it opens the door to communication from your employees that will prove to be an invaluable aid in the success of your business.

8

Secret 6: Power to the People

Power used absolutely diminishes. Power shared absolutely expands.

Power is a fascinating concept. I would venture that more books have been written about power than even its siren twin sister, money. In fact, a quick Google search turns up 849 million hits for power and *only* 762 million hits for money.

The concept of power permeates every interaction of humanity (and even beyond that to include Republicans). Since the two humans first met, they have been willing to do almost anything to gain power over others. Once tasted, people will do even more to keep power. (Joseph Stalin's proclivity to execute anyone who might be even the slightest threat to his power is a good example of this, but we will leave that tale for the history books.) Over time, societies have been stratified by the lines of power. Virtually every organization—schools, businesses, governments, and even families—exist in a hierarchal structure, largely divided by the *powerful* and the *powerless*. (That's especially true if husbands are included in the equation.)

There is a general belief that one primordial drive of the entrepreneur is the acquisition and use of power. Feeling powerless in large companies, they move on, seeking their own power. The cartoon of the overly corpulent bombastic entrepreneur sitting at his desk amassing power is all too familiar. This is yet another myth about the characteristics of the real entrepreneur.

Lust for Power

Power is sought after, stockpiled, used, and abused more by bureaucrats than any other individuals. For the bureaucrat, power is the reward for playing and surviving within the system. Bureaucrats garner neither respect nor trust from those trapped in the system, so they fall back on gaining and using power (no matter how trivial) to validate their very existence. This mindset is compounded by the reality that very few bureaucrats have any real power outside the bureaucratic system.

While power struggles are an accepted everyday occurrence in a bureaucracy (they are one of the tell-tale signs of a bureaucracy), there are rarely such shenanigans in an entrepreneurial culture. This conundrum exists because in a bureaucracy most forces are in conflict and power becomes a measure of relevance, while in an entrepreneurial culture interests are parallel and the power of the group, not the individual, is the sign of success.

It is not a sin to seek or achieve power. Problems surface when we worship at the altar of power as bureaucrats do, so that they melt into this ultimate vice as described by the poet Shelley in his lengthy narrative poem, *Queen Mab* (1813):

Power, like a desolating pestilence,

Pollutes whate'er it touches . . .

Somewhere between the vice and virtue of power is fertile ground for entrepreneurs to advance their visions and careers by learning the real secret to acquiring and using power: *The way to acquire power is to share power.* The more power is shared the more it will grow.

Please understand, when discussing power, I'm not necessarily referring to the horrific power wielded by presidents, emperors, or kings—not to mention spouses. Power is relative. For the purpose of our discussions, power is defined as having the ability to make a difference and an impact on the outcome of an objective. Using this definition, we need not be corporate titans or political kingpins to wield power.

Bureaucrats who already possess power spend much of their time scheming to prevent others from obtaining it. The cruel irony is that because they already have power, they have the control to establish the rules dealing with the acquisition of power. Not surprisingly, this makes it quite difficult for the *have-nots* to become the *haves* and for those who are powerless to become powerful.

I would not dare to be presumptuous enough to put myself in the class of great thinkers (except maybe in my own mind), but it seems to me that all bureaucrats miss the point. You don't make yourself more powerful by reducing the power of others or transferring power to yourself—you do the exact opposite. The way to deal with power is not to consolidate it, but to figure out how to create more of it to spread around. If you acquire power as bureaucrats do by withholding it from others, they will resent it and fight you. The entrepreneur understands how to leverage power in a way that creates new power so that the conflict is eliminated.

A Page from My Files

Recently I was a discouraged, firsthand observer of the destruction that can be caused by the bureaucratic approach to power. I worked with the head of North American operations for a large, international company who could be the poster child for corporate bureaucracy. He met the classic definition of a bureaucrat run amok in a bureaucracy and exhibited the famous *I pattern* of most bureaucrats—incompetent, insecure, and intellectually dishonest. (He once called me aside after I had given a speech at a meeting and complained that I had not given him enough credit for his efforts.) Like many bureaucrats, he made the decision long ago to place power above principle.

Under the guise of improving efficiency and reducing costs, this guy consolidated many of the functions of diverse companies under the control of a central holding company, which is run by him. Functions, such as information technology, legal, human resources, finance, and even marketing have been consolidated under his control. Clearly this is a classic bureaucratic power grab. He even compounded the negative effects of this power play by doing what most bureaucrats in power do—surrounding himself with a staff of individuals whose primary talent is the ability or willingness to cater to his ego and wishes.

This is another interesting lesson to learn. Bureaucrats invariably surround themselves with people who they think are less talented than they are and who thus present no threat. Anyone who may pose a threat is browbeaten into submission. Alternatively, entrepreneurs seek to surround themselves with people who are *more* talented than they are, and they encourage these people to challenge them.

The actions taken by this bureaucrat were not only foolhardy because the purported expense savings will never be achieved (managing, not cutting expenses is the way to build a company), but he has carved the very heart and soul out of the various organizations.

Bureaucracies Strip Employees of Motivation

When a bureaucracy strips employees of the power to make a difference, makes them feel that they cannot add value and are indeed powerless, then employees lose all interest and motivation. It's not bad enough that members of the organization become demoralized; the talented ones are driven away and those who remain are there only to collect paychecks. As another observer with knowledge of the situation commented, "This guy's actions are creating a true corporate meltdown."

Of course, many would not fault this guy because he is just playing by the accepted bureaucratic system rules—and playing them quite well. Unfortunately, if history is any lesson, costs will actually increase, efficiency will deteriorate, and the value of the organization will erode as it sinks into the abyss of institutional bureaucracy. But at least this guy will have his power.

Share the Power

Contrary to the existing bureaucratic philosophy, the way to gain personal power is to empower others. The secret known by entrepreneurs is that the amount of power you possess will be magnified and leveraged in incremental proportion to the power you give to others. Only the one *with* power can grant power, so the more power you grant to others, the more power you gain. It also follows that when those in an organization—an entrepreneurial culture—are empowered, then the organization becomes geometrically more powerful. The bureaucratic system breaks power down into individual cells that defuse the organization's power to perform. The entrepreneur knows that the way to beat the system is to coalesce power in the hands of the people to focus the efforts of the culture.

Lessons from History

History offers some wonderful validations of this approach. During the Cold War, did anything seem stronger or more implacable than the bureaucratic political, economic, and social stranglehold the former Soviet Union and the countries of Eastern Europe held over their citizens? It was difficult to imagine that anything—short of nuclear war— could break the iron grip of these governments over their people. The government held all the power and the people none.

Both in politics and in business, the *appearance* of power is almost always stronger than the reality. A dictator can remain in power only as long as he can maintain the appearance that he possesses total power. In fact, power—any level of power—is a very thin veneer of gloss held in place by either trust or fear. Once these elements disappear, then the hold on power becomes tenuous. Whenever masses of people share the same vision and rise up in parallel (as in an entrepreneurial culture), the existing power of a government or a bureaucracy becomes helpless to keep them under control.

The Polish government (despite what Gerald Ford believed) was as repressive as any government in the Eastern block. The Polish people had no power and barely more than potatoes to eat. Yet, the walls began to crack and crumble when an obscure and uneducated Polish shipyard worker by the name of Lech Walesa began to convince his comrades that they had the power to make things better for themselves and their country.

Rather than trying to gain power playing by the rules of the system, namely joining the party and supporting the status quo till it was his turn, Walesa gained power by rejecting and cheating on the rules of the system. His secret was that rather than seeking power for himself, he sought power for the people. In the end, Walesa became powerful—and eventually the president of Poland—by empowering other people.

Entrepreneurial Cultures Share Power

Building an entrepreneurial culture may not be quite as grandiose as overthrowing repressive governments (although I know some that should be) or changing the course of the world forever, but the very same principles apply. Here are some specific examples of how an entrepreneur can gain power by sharing power.

First of all, think of empowering people in the context of a scavenger hunt. If you are leading the game, you come up with the items to be collected, the time frame, and the limits of the search. Once these have been agreed on and the tasks distributed, the teams are free to decide what course of action is needed to accomplish the objective. As with an entrepreneurial culture, anyone playing the game is given the objectives, but the power to determine how they are to be achieved is left in the hands of the participants.

The entrepreneur also looks at power sharing from another perspective. Bureaucrats can generally be thought of as *micromanagers*. For them, details are more important than the objective. They retain the power of those details for themselves and hover over the workers showing neither trust nor respect as they smother the workers' ability to make decisions. On the other hand, entrepreneurs understand a little secret that goes beyond the bureaucrat's ability to comprehend. And that simple secret is: *If you don't care about the decision, allow others to make it.*

The entrepreneur is always involved in defining the vision, outlining objectives, and delineating guidelines, but once these are in place, he has the ability to step back and allow others to have the power of making specific decisions. If the objective is to drive from Chicago to Atlanta and you are almost out of gas, does it really make any difference which gas station you stop at to fill up? The entrepreneur understands that very few decisions made in business are life and death; however, he reserves the right to make some decisions himself or at least the right to review the recommended decision. For all other decisions, he is willing to step back and empower others.

Not by the Hair of My Chiny Chin Chin

Power is so sacred to the bureaucrat that he is unwilling to release even one vestige of it. The bureaucrat is like a tribal witch doctor who seeks to retain his mystical power by not allowing others to enter the temple of the gods. The entrepreneur is confident enough with himself and his people to give up the power to make decisions. This is one of the secrets that enables the entrepreneur to beat the system.

How You Can Build Power

Building your own power as an entrepreneur by empowering others is a three-step process. One, communicate; two, respect; and three, trust. I have learned over the years that—no matter what level of power you may have—your power will be enhanced and strengthened if your efforts are used to enforce those simple points to share your power with others.

When a management philosophy employs constant transparent communication, shows a need and respect for the talents of employees, and trusts them to do the right thing, then an environment is created that is fertile for the growth of the leader's power and influence. This is a simple philosophy that works at the mailroom level as well as it works in the palace. Experience has convinced me that people in their own world, whether it's large or small, can be more powerful if their first objective is to empower others in that world.

We mention this in other parts of the book, but the first secret to sharing power is to break the system's rule on the accumulation, control, and dissemination of information. Bureaucrats deem that information is an expression of (quite rightly) power. The bureaucrat has sworn a blood oath that, because information is power, it is to be protected and parceled out only to those in the power club. Recognizing the relationship of information to power, the bureaucrat hoards it while the entrepreneur shares it.

This attitude is no different from that in the pre–Civil War South where citizens were prohibited from teaching slaves to read and write. Lawmakers knew that literacy was power. Accordingly, a literate slave was usually a contradiction in terms. Sometimes it seems as if bureaucrats would like to see this philosophy come back in vogue. Then again when it comes to dealing with employees, most bureaucrats act as if the times have not changed.

The entrepreneur respects the power of information, but, unlike the bureaucrat, he or she also understands that if you keep it to yourself or try to bury it like a treasure, then information becomes very much like an unused battery hidden away in a drawer slowly losing its power. There is more to breaking the system's power rules than just sharing specific facts. It also relates to the types of communication given to those you are trying to empower.

Power in the corporate world is the guy in the corner office on the top floor who has two secretaries; you have to fight through an armada of gatekeepers to see this person. If that's going on in the company where you work, you're getting a definite signal—the person in the big corner office on the top floor has tons of clout and wants to keep it that way. That is the wrong signal to give.

Is This What Power Looks Like?

If you visited LifeUSA or Allianz Life when I was CEO, you would not have found a secretary (or the politically correct term *administrative assistant*) guarding my office. The door was open and you could walk right in. My office was cluttered with homey artifacts that put employees and visitors at ease. The signal I was sending was that power comes from different sources or different approaches.

I wanted to send employees (owners) an unmistakable message: You are the important, powerful people. Employees make or break a company. They will work hard because of the respect you've given them. As a result of their work, you can become more powerful than you ever would have by hiding on the penthouse level.

The fashionable thing for business books to espouse these days is the philosophy of *people empowerment*. They argue rightly that empowerment is the path to success, but they tiptoe around the crux of the notion without putting real teeth into their actions.

What they don't quite understand is that the measure of your power is not based on your title, but on the percentage of power you share. Learning to share real power with those critical to the success of the organization is crucial.

Don't Talk—Listen

The simple technique of listening is one of the most basic secrets an entrepreneur can use to share power with people. A basic difference between the management style of a bureaucrat and an entrepreneur is that the bureaucrat tells and the entrepreneur listens.

You know how frustrating it can be to sit down with a boss who only wants to talk about his issues? You can sit with some people for an hour, and for most of that time all they do is tell you their stories. What does that say to you? Obviously, they care more about themselves than about you. They are showing no interest and worse—no respect for you. You may have had something important to discuss, but after trying on numerous occasions to break in, you just give up and let them drone on—and by that time you have tuned them out.

When you are genuinely willing to listen to the thoughts and ideas of employees, they are empowered, respect is communicated, and trust is established. Empowering communication is as much listening as it is talking. Creating an environment that encourages openness and listening makes us the beneficiary (notice I just can't get away from the insurance business) of valuable information on a constant basis. At the same time, it also constantly signals our respect and belief in the power of the person offering the information.

I was fortunate to stumble onto the idea of gaining by simply showing respect for others when I moved out of the core at State Mutual. While that act of moving out of the core dealt with intimidation, it was also a lesson in gaining power. My move to the general work area sent a message to the people I worked with that they were more important than the executives I left behind. It transferred a sense of power to them to know that someone who had power in the company (at least more than they did) chose to be among them. This gave them an access to power they had not experienced before and made them feel (and in fact be) more powerful.

This form of respect from the leader resulted in increased effort to reciprocate the shared power and respect. Soon our department was able to do more work, and do it more quickly and more efficiently than other areas. This small example did not have a huge impact on the company and certainly not on the world, but it did make a mark on me. Slowly, it became apparent that the department—and the people along with it—had become a powerful force in the company simply because of these small steps toward empowerment. In turn, I became more powerful and influential in the company than would have been possible by trying to keep control of the power while my office remained in the core.

One activity at LifeUSA served as a wonderful example for employee empowerment. It was called *work simplification* and involved a group of employees from different disciplines getting together to look for ways to improve the activity and productivity of the company. The processes that were examined could be anything from the processing of applications to the distribution of payroll. The idea was—as the company grew larger—to discover simpler or more efficient ways of running the company. Employees were not assigned to these committees, they volunteered. And, we had employees standing in line to participate. Why? Because they knew their recommendations would be taken seriously and that they had the power to impact the company. The power of these employees working together made me and other managers that much more powerful because of the power we had shared.

The ultimate example of power sharing was the concept of employee ownership at LifeUSA. If ownership is power, then sharing both is the ultimate in empowering employees. How can anyone have more power or feel more empowered, than when they are true owners of the enterprise?

These examples of empowering others demonstrate that it is possible to empower others—and increase your own power—but it does not have to be as dramatic as making all employees owners of the company. That certainly is one way and it might be the best way, but it may not always be possible. The rules may say that power shared is power lost, but the reality is that power shared is power enhanced.

Summary of the Secret

Gaining power is one of the most fundamental motivators of human interaction. With centuries of history as a base and generation upon generation of effort, an almost genetically inspired system has developed regarding the acquisition, use, and preservation of power. Most of the rules the system has developed for dealing with power were well intended at the time of their enactment. The trouble is that they have been corrupted over time. Instead of being a path for others to follow, the rules have become bureaucratized in an effort to protect the status quo and the status of those who *have,* while keeping those who *don't have* from having.

In the bureaucratic world of today, power is stockpiled; you hoard it for your own use only. The bureaucrat keeps all the vestiges of power that give him a feeling of status and privilege. A powerless person is seen as no threat to the system. The secret to the entrepreneur's ability to beat the system is that he or she seeks ways to give power to the people—to empower the powerless.

I can understand why people with power seek every way possible to squirrel it away and protect it. Those in the system believe that power is a measure of their own worth (maybe the only one) and so they have been taught to protect power as dearly as life itself. Entrepreneurs advocate an approach that is as different as night and day. They believe the secret to beating the system is not to usurp power, but rather to create new power for all.

What's difficult for bureaucrats to comprehend is that if you take less, you will get more. A more cohesive, productive business, like rising tides, raises the boats of all employees. And it works on all business levels whether it's a sole proprietorship with three employees, a department manager with 25 employees, or a corporate titan with thousands.

The entrepreneur understands that amazing levels of power can be created when he implements techniques that empower others. An entrepreneurial culture is like a nuclear reactor. The chain reaction of atoms working together does not use power—it creates huge amounts of new power.

The irony is that we are talking about stuff that is not rocket science. It is not hard to do when you make it a way of life. The entrepreneur recognizes and understands exactly why it is important to give power to the people. The bottom line is that entrepreneurs know that the benefit is ultimately their own.

It is my hope that in this chapter, as in every chapter of this book, you come away with the mindset that there is no simple one, two, three explanation to building an entrepreneurial culture in our bureaucratic world. There is no formula that says, "On Tuesday you do this, and on Wednesday you do that." Rather, you should develop a mindset of being willing to challenge the status quo of the system. One of the most disarming facts about being an entrepreneur is that virtually all of the principles of entrepreneurialism are so easy to put in place. And it's the very ease of the effort that often stymies and confuses the bureaucrat.

Imagine that all you have to do to gain power is to simply share the power you already possess. Put your employees or team members on your side by inviting them to share in your company's (or your department's) power. It's a concept that's almost Biblical—a simple business Golden Rule: give to others and they will give back to you tenfold.

9

Secret 7: Become a Trust Builder

Trust is the most underrated aspect of an organizational culture. The presence of trust makes any effort possible. The absence of trust corrodes from within until nothing is possible.

One of the best compliments a business leader can receive is to have the people he works with say, "I would follow him blindly, anywhere, anytime." The entrepreneur understands that no matter how transparent he may wish to be, no matter how much he communicates and explains there are going to be times when total disclosure is not possible and times when some people are simply not going to understand his actions. It is times like these that the true entrepreneur can move forward confidently and seamlessly knowing that his group will not only follow, but support his decisions. The entrepreneur is self-assured because he understands the secret power of trust. In essence, trust becomes a guide dog for entrepreneurial cultures. Even more important, the entrepreneur knows the secrets to building trust.

Trust bestows an operational freedom on the entrepreneur that is never enjoyed by bureaucratic leaders. Trust in an entrepreneurial culture is different from trust in a marriage or the trust we place in a pilot when we board an airliner. In fact, I would even disassociate the concept of entrepreneurial trust from ethical action, which is the idea we normally associate with trust. Not that the entrepreneur can build trust without being ethical, but in this context trust has a different nuance. Trust in an entrepreneurial culture is about many things, but mostly it is about being able to have faith in a leader's consistency.

Building Business Trust

One of the secrets to building business trust is consistency: being the same today as you were yesterday and will be tomorrow. This is fairly natural for the entrepreneur because he is focused on the vision of the objective and while techniques may be adjusted, that vision never changes. Consistency also applies to personal style. It does not mean that the leader has to be a saint, but it does mean that you can't be a saint one day and the incarnation of the devil the next. Building trust starts with the consistency of the leader, even if consistency means that he is consistently a jerk. Developing trust for a leader does not mean that his followers necessarily like him, but it does mean that they can count on his consistency.

When it comes to managing a culture, consistency has an even more practical application. Entrepreneurs know the simple secret of standards. If you are going to set a standard, stand by it. You can't engender trust in an organization if with great fanfare your company announces a mission statement and then immediately takes action contrary to that statement. Imagine announcing a wonderful stock option plan and then your employees discovering that the big boys got to cherry-pick their own option date to put more cash into their pockets. What a horrible way to build trust among the rank and file.

It is no wonder that trust levels in bureaucracies are notoriously low when bureaucrats are famous for saying one thing and doing another. Bureaucrats do not place a high level of importance on establishing trust with employees because they don't think it is necessary. Why do they need trust when they have power? Bureaucrats have a why-should-I-worry-about-employees-trusting-me attitude. I have heard them say, "The job of the employee is to follow my orders, and I trust they will do it—but I really don't trust them very much."

In contrast, entrepreneurs know a secret: Trust is their get-out-of-jail-free card they can play when they need one. When an entrepreneur who has built high levels of trust asks employees to do something, they comply, even if they don't understand the reason, because past experience tells them it is okay to follow—even blindly.

The trust levels in an organization ultimately boil down to the simple old axiom, "Fool me once, shame on you. Fool me twice, shame on me."

A Fitting Example

As consultant to a very large company, I was witness to a classic example of the negative fallout that occurs when this attitude is present. I was able to observe the destructive results of bureaucratic management imposed by one of the senior executives. Whenever a situation developed, such as an employee asking for approval of a project or when he directed some action, the executive would always say, "I'll back you all the way on this." He would then go on to say, "I will put my reputation on the line for you." Of course, you know the rest of the story.

From past experience, the employees knew this guy could not be trusted and when push came to shove he could not be counted on. In fact, it became kind of a joke among the employees. They would say, "Having support from this guy was like the kiss of death." They always cringed whenever he told them how much he supported them. Clearly the guy had lost any element of trust with his employees, and you can imagine just how the productivity of the divisions under him suffered. This was a classic case of a bureaucrat not understanding (or respecting) the need for trust within an organization. The loss of productivity, value, and opportunity in a situation like this is incalculable.

Without trust, any venture will suffer. Productivity sags. Employee morale is low. And the competition for good personnel can leave the organization struggling with the high cost of employee turnover. And we're not talking peanuts here. Employee turnover costs can be huge. Nationally, the average annual employee turnover rate for all companies is 12 percent. One study by the Center for Community and Economic Development found that "75 percent of the demand for new employees is simply to replace workers who have left the company." Of course, not all employees leave a company because of corporate mistrust. They leave for many reasons. But corporate mistrust is a major progenitor.

Origins of Corporate Mistrust

Naturally, corporate mistrust can occur in businesses of all sizes, but it is particularly prevalent in bureaucratic cultures. Bureaucratic cultures tend to limit the accumulation of power and information to the few, the *top brass,* so to speak. Bureaucrats think that by hoarding information they hoard greater power. The result is a vacuum of information among the rank and file—the coin of the realm in building trust.

The result? Secrecy breeds suspicion. In a bureaucratic culture, people don't know whom to trust. They don't know from one day to the next what the game plan is or what rules apply. This causes more rumors to fly than birds heading south in the winter.

Entrepreneurs Build Trust

The traditional rules of the bureaucratic system do not require trust to be built between the leader and the followers because the followers are supposed to follow and obey. People are being paid to do their jobs. Trust is not an element deemed critical to doing a job. This philosophy is outdated today and only serves to entrench bureaucracy in a culture of distrust.

If employees are the operators of the *business machine,* then the secret to keeping that system well oiled and operating at peak efficiency is trust. The entrepreneur understands that if a leader loses trust, then no matter what the objective is, it is unlikely that others will follow. If employees who work for you trust you and believe that you really will take care of their best interests, they are not only mentally free to do the jobs that need to be done, but they demonstrate that trust by pushing *you* up the ladder ahead of them. When you attempt to lead without simultaneously building trust from constituent followers, you write yourself a prescription for a difficult time.

Secrets to Building Entrepreneurial Trust

The first step to building entrepreneurial trust is to recognize that it is a process not a procedure. True deep-seated trust does not come overnight, it comes over time, and it cannot be mandated. Sure, most of us are trusting by nature. We are willing to give people the benefit of the doubt, but our depth of trust is limited after the first time it is broken.

The entrepreneur begins the process by setting standards for the organization. These standards must be clear, concise, and rigorously followed. These standards are components of the ultimate objective of the organization; they offer a clear understanding of what is and what is not acceptable practice and how people should expect to be treated. The standards set by a leader are the front phalanx in the effort to build trust. The standards are really a set of inviolate principles upon which the organization is managed and led. And by inviolate, I *do* mean inviolate; they do not change.

The irony is that members of an organization do not have to agree with the standards to build trust. They only need to know what the standards are and that they will be consistently enforced at all times so that they know where to stand and how to behave. (If for any reason a member of an organization is uncomfortable with the standards in place, it is logical for him to exit and find an environment more suitable to his comfort level.)

In a true entrepreneurial culture, everybody knows the standards, and all employees know where the company is and where the company is going. Employees know the inviolate rules. They also know that to stay within a business's culture they have to live by the standards and not outside them.

This doesn't mean that management is totally inflexible. An entrepreneur is always flexible about *how* to do something but is never flexible about *what* to do.

Rules of Engagement

To introduce flexibility into the management of an organization without violating the established standards, a set of *rules of engagement* must be established. The rules of engagement are a set of guidelines about what the organization will and will not do to achieve its objectives. Within these rules of engagement, employees are empowered to make independent decisions and to do what has to be done to reach objectives. And that is another secret to building trust that entrepreneurs understand—the more the members of an organization are empowered, the more they trust their managers.

For example, let's say you are running an insurance company with a vision to become the leader in providing products for retirement. In this case, your inviolate standard is codified so that the company only markets products that help people accumulate funds for retirement. It's as simple as it is enforceable.

So, if someone comes in with a great plan to sell billions of dollars worth of term insurance—which only provides a benefit if people die—then the response should always be no. If you change gears, if you stutter, backslide, or give in to the pressures to change the vision, trust begins to break down because people in the organization can't rely on the standards being the standards.

The design of the retirement product to be sold could provide us with another example of a rule not to be violated. The rule might be, "We will develop and market products based only on value and not price." Under such a scenario, the rules of engagement could be that the company will sell to individuals rather than groups. With these standards, principles, and rules of engagement in place, members of the organization are empowered to develop any type of retirement product based on value added and sold to any individuals they desire.

When true entrepreneurial management trust is established, employees can rely on the guidelines remaining constant. Plus, by allowing them to decide how to make the magic happen (within accepted guidelines), you enhance mutual trust and respect.

This never happens within a bureaucratic organization because standards are constantly shifting. Bureaucrats never empower employees to work independently within the system.

Create Employee/Management Trust

The most effective way to build trust in the entrepreneurial workplace is by working together to generate mutual respect. It would be nice if trust could be built using simple gimmicks, but it cannot. Great company picnics are nice and so is the company bowling team, but they'll fall far short of building the trust you need to be a true entrepreneur. Teamwork, honesty, and fair play are what you need.

How do entrepreneurs build that trust? In an entrepreneurial culture, the members know how the leader feels about the major issues. And how do they know? It's a secret as simple as 1-2-3:

1. The entrepreneur communicates clearly what he is going to do.

2. Then the entrepreneur always does what he said he was going to do.

3. Finally, the entrepreneur does 1 and 2 again and again and again.

For the entrepreneur, this translates into seeking ways to be open and honest about all company operations and to be fair and consistent in his treatment of all employees. What are some of the techniques entrepreneurs use to accomplish this objective?

Trust is a two-way street. Entrepreneurs want members of the culture to know about management perspectives, but they also want to know what *their members think.* To find out, entrepreneurs take many different steps such as:

- Having an open-door policy where employees have the opportunity to offer information, questions, or suggestions.
- Taking time to talk with your workers. Making it a point to get out on the plant floor to rub shoulders and ask questions.
- Asking employees how it's going and what they're thinking.
- Finding out what information employees want to know and then telling them whenever possible.

These may be simple and easy steps, but it is amazing how many bureaucrats do not even make the attempt.

Trust Is Not Easily Developed

As I said earlier, the problem is that you cannot command trust. Leaders must earn it. Over time, entrepreneurs discover that the most effective way to build trust with people is the simple process of communication and transparency. Entrepreneurs are always totally open with others regarding the issues, challenges, objectives, and plans of the business. Entrepreneurs are willing to take the risk to trust people with their future and the success of the company. Employees realize this and learn to trust management. Entrepreneurs know a simple little secret: The more they trust their people, the more *they* are trusted. Bureaucrats rarely command trust because they rarely offer trust.

I cannot stress enough that *trust is engendered through openness, integrity, clarity of expression, and constancy*. It's a product of saying what you're going to do, and then doing it, without changing course.

This goes for bad news as well as good news. If entrepreneurs have some bad news, they are open about it and don't sugarcoat or gloss over the inconvenient truth.

An Entrepreneur Who Learned This Lesson Early

I was on a consulting assignment with a new company and was impressed by the way the entrepreneur was so open and evenhanded regarding the information he provided to employees. In fact, he almost went overboard making sure his employees had a full understanding of the risks facing the company.

You have probably heard of the term *burn rate*. This is a calculation that companies make to determine how long they can stay in business based on their current revenue and expense using their current levels of available capital. This tool is most often used by start-up ventures, but sometimes even big companies are forced to make the analysis. Both General Motors and Ford Motor companies have been forced to report burn rates.

Anyway, this start-up entrepreneur not only kept a close eye on the burn rate, he also posted that information on a chart so that all employees were aware of the situation. This chart was updated with the latest calculation each month. This was a gutsy act. Fear is the first risk. If employees see that, unless things improve, the company could be out of business within a year, then they could be out pounding the pavement. This entrepreneur believed it was better to trust the employees and include them in the process than to try to hide the facts from them. After all, he recognized these were the people who would have the most to do with the survival and success of the company.

Tools for Trust Building

As you have learned from reading this chapter (if you are still with me), the effort to build trust within an organization is multifaceted and requires continuous consistent actions in every process of the organization. And it should; trust is not something that can just be turned on and off.

The entrepreneur knows that part of building trust is assuring that when employees commit to a project, they have the tools to complete it. If they are going to go out on a limb for you, they want to be comfortable knowing their leader will be there with the safety equipment. Trust evaporates fairly quickly if employees accept an assignment only to discover that the tools to do the job are missing and the boss is off on the next project.

The entrepreneur sends a simple message to his troops, "Step out and do this for me and I've got your back!" While the members of the organization put their heads down and plow forward on the project, the entrepreneur is there to provide support and cover. Should something go wrong, the employees are confident their leader will be right there with them. This natural relationship in entrepreneurial cultures results in a reservoir of trust, but is rarely seen in bureaucratic cultures.

Sharing Builds Trust

There is another secret the entrepreneur uses to build the bonds of trust within his organization. The entrepreneur conscientiously and consistently shares the success of the project with everyone who participated. In entrepreneurial cultures, victories are always shared. In fact, the entrepreneur often goes out of his way to pass credit along to those who do the work. At the same time, the entrepreneur takes most of the blame if the project fails. It's not that the entrepreneur ignores errors. On the contrary, the entrepreneur uses these errors to instruct, not to condemn. There is a difference between a project failing and the commission of errors. The entrepreneur accepts the failure (after all it was his project) and teaches from the errors.

When a member of an organization is confident that his leader will clearly explain the job to be done, is consistent in what he wants, provides the support and tools needed to complete the project, and then is willing to pass along credit for the success, a trust is established that allows the employee to confidently move forward.

Do What You Say

There is no faster way to lose trust and credibility than going back on your word or weaseling around commitments. I'll give you an example of where exigencies could push you into changing your management posture and losing trust. When Allianz SE purchased LifeUSA, they allowed us to institute a new incentive system into the merged company, rather than what Allianz worldwide was using. The new plan was a duplicate of the plan used at LifeUSA.

When we put that system in place, the Allianz employees couldn't really understand it. It had no credibility because, previously, the only people who had ever gotten a bonus at Allianz Life were senior executives. Does this sound familiar?

This plan was introduced at a time when there were clearly underperforming divisions at Allianz Life. Due to this situation, it was obvious that some departments would earn a bonus while others would not.

At the end of the year, those departments that had done well got bonuses, bigger bonuses than they had ever seen. Those who didn't do well got nothing. But here's the kicker—the management of the groups that got nothing came to me and said, "You can't do that. We have to get something. It's not fair. These people are getting their bonuses and we are not."

Yet, I had to say, "That's too bad. That was the deal. That is what we communicated. And I can't change it now. A deal is a deal." Your heart may go out to those who failed to perform. It may implore you to give in. But shifting gears at this stage is a surefire formula for breaking faith.

While this outcome did not make everyone happy, it did make a point. Those from the old Allianz could see we were adamant about this plan; we did what we promised and despite the lack of a bonus their trust began to grow. The attitude of most was, "You know, they did what they said they were going to do. Maybe I didn't get a bonus, but we didn't perform well, and I know that. So I guarantee that next year we are going to perform well." Those who did receive a bonus felt, "Hey, this thing works. Not only did we get a bonus, but it also got spread equitably among the people who were involved. So I am going to work harder next year."

But remember, the point here is not about money. It is about consistency. It is about honesty. It is about credibility. Employees received a clear message that produced the kind of trustful thinking that I wanted. Employees would think to themselves, "You know, this is a different kind of deal. I used to believe that I could work my ass off and nobody would care. So after a while of thankless busting my ass, I just don't want to work as hard anymore. But now, if I work my ass off, management will see that. They will appreciate that. They will respect that. It is not the money I want so much as it is the acknowledgment that I am a contributing team member." Trust was beginning to build. In the years that followed, bonuses were larger than they had ever been, and everyone who added value got to share in the value.

Summary of the Secret

Entrepreneurs never discount the value of trust. Trust or the lack of trust can be a powerful force. When present, it can free the culture to accomplish great things, and when it is missing, it can eat away at the very soul of an organization and paralyze efforts.

Remember that old personality question: Would you rather be liked or respected? The entrepreneur always picks respect. The entrepreneur craves the trust that respect generates. He knows that without it, very little else can be accomplished. The bureaucrat gives short shrift to trust because he does not care if people trust him, only that they do what they are told.

If you want to succeed as a true entrepreneur you must begin by being a trust builder.

10

Secret 8: Sharing Wealth Increases Wealth

The real value of reward is the just recognition of the value added.

In an earlier chapter, we learned that the first and most important secret to creating an entrepreneurial culture in a bureaucratic world is to constantly seek to build parallel interests. When all business interests are aligned in parallel, the individual interests of many are directed powerfully toward the welfare of the whole. Parallel interests means that the interests of management and the interests of employees are aligned. Employees have no reason to believe that management would do anything that is not in their best interests, and management has no reason to believe that employees would to anything that is not in the best interests of the organization.

The secret discussed in this chapter deals with properly rewarding people who are in parallel, so that they are motivated to remain in parallel. This secret is based on a simple truism: *Those who have the ability to add value to an organization will be encouraged to do so if they are allowed to share in the value created.*

Seems obvious and mundane doesn't it? The idea is so basic and simple that it would be difficult to find someone who would disagree with a statement like that. Right? Well, frankly, many people do disagree. Bureaucrats believe employees should be paid specifically for the work they do for a company. Let's call that *task work*. Employees in bureaucratic organizations are paid fairly for the tasks they perform, but are offered little other interaction or motivation to do more than their duty. Bureaucracies can sincerely claim they are fair to employees because they offer a good working environment, provide equal opportunity, and offer pay that is competitive. The bureaucrat is comfortable with this rationalization because from his perspective, the employee is simply a task doer, not a *value adder*.

With such a philosophy in place, the bureaucrat has neither a guilty conscience nor motivation to include most employees in stock option, profit sharing, or other plans based on individual performance. Because employees are simply task doers, there is no need to inform or communicate with them beyond the latest increase in health plan co-pay benefits. As a result, employees have no incentive to do anything more than their jobs. There are no real parallel interests.

The philosophy in an entrepreneurial organization is different. Yes, the entrepreneurial organization also pays for task work, offers good benefits, and a good working environment, just like the bureaucracy. However, the secret to the success of the entrepreneurial culture is a deep-seated belief that employees can be more than just task doers. The entrepreneur views employees as lynchpins to the success of the company. The entrepreneur seeks to persuade employees to see their personal interests in line with the interests of the company by creating an environment that motivates employees to go beyond the feeling of *having a job* to the feeling of *owning their job*. The entrepreneur understands that the way to accomplish this is through actions that equitably share the increased value created by the employees with the employees. The trick is to find the most effective way to achieve this objective.

Sharing Rewards with Stock Ownership

Certainly the easiest, cleanest way to share rewards is through actual stock ownership. When employees *own* part of the business, they take better care of it, just as we take better care of a home we own rather than lease.

At LifeUSA, we felt that employee ownership was so important to the success of the company that employees were actually *required* to purchase stock in the company. All employees were obligated to allocate 10 percent of their gross pay to purchase LifeUSA stock. It was, as venture capitalists like to say, *putting skin in the game.* (Of course, to maintain true parallel interests, the employees must own the same class of stock purchased at the same price as the executives.) Entrepreneurs understand instinctively that the best way for everyone to have skin in the game is for everyone to be a real owner.

Bill Gates with Microsoft is another great example of an entrepreneur who understands the value of putting employees in parallel with the company by using stock ownership. It is now part of American business lore how many multimillionaires were made at Microsoft. Do you really believe that Microsoft would have become as successful as it has without the concept of employee stock ownership? If you do, don't tell Bill Gates. Here is another interesting point in the entrepreneur/employee relationship. While Bill Gates made billions and employees *only* made millions, you never hear employees begrudging Gates his billions. Why? Because at Microsoft, every employee had an equitable chance to participate in the success of the company. Not so in bureaucratic businesses. We constantly hear of employees expressing frustration and dissatisfaction with the level of CEO pay because they get no share in the value they add.

But not all businesses can allow actual employee stock ownership (actually, that is not true, but it is the accepted myth so we'll go with it). People who want to be entrepreneurs in these companies need to create practical strategies that allow value to be shared in different ways. Even if it is not practical to share actual ownership of the company with employees, it is possible in any size company to create the feeling of ownership by fostering the concept of parallel interests. Among these, the proper use of paycheck strategies, bonuses, and other similar financial rewards that put the employee in parallel with management and other stakeholders. All are designed to give the employee a tangible reason to put forth superior efforts. They all suggest on a continuing basis an elemental principle of entrepreneurism: it pays to make the effort to add value beyond task work because you will be respected and recognized, while sharing in the value you helped create.

Pay for Performance

As I wrote in my earlier book, *Cheat to Win,* employee compensation is an effective way to promote shared value. However, sometime in the foggy history of corporate governance, an obscure management guru specializing in the esoteric study of corporate time and motion came up with the rule on compensation philosophy that is now in place at virtually every major company in the United States. The rule is: *Employees should be paid for the value of the job, not the value the individual brings to the job.*

This rule relies on the use of grade and time levels of compensation. The federal government is the poster child for this bit of regimentation, which should tell you a great deal about its effectiveness. In government service your public relations job is a Public Information Specialist G-1035-14. Or if you're a doctor, you are labeled as a Supervisory Medical Officer GS-602-15. It's no wonder the government pays $300 for a screwdriver and gives away a week's pay for a toilet seat.

The underlying idea is to place a range of value on the job based on how long the employee has been in the position and the value assigned to the position by some geeky human resources consultant. No matter the extent of real value an employee may add to an organization—all employees are compensated at a predetermined value for the job, not the value added by the individual. In addition, once employees reach the top of the scale, they are blocked from any future increase in compensation in that job.

Is this dumb or what? Think about it. If an employee has been with the company long enough to reach the top of his or her pay grade, isn't it logical to assume that this person knows the job better than anyone else in the company, and that the experience of this individual may be adding significantly more value than other employees in the same job? Yet to receive an increase in compensation (other than cost-of-living increases), this employee must resign and move to a new job. Sure, it may be a job that pays more money, but one in which the employee has little experience and can add less value. What sense does this make for the company? Wouldn't these employees be more inclined to work hard if they were being paid for the value added by their experience rather than just time in grade?

Adding Parallel to Your Shop

LifeUSA developed a pay-grade system that established certain ranges based on the minimum expectations for the job. If an employee did the job but little more—simply went through the motions—he or she received the basic wage. However, another factor in the compensation system was to measure and pay for *extra value* brought to the job by a talented person doing more than was expected, which added value to the company. And this extra value had no maximum level.

The result was that two employees slotted in the same job for the same amount of time could be paid significantly different amounts. The theory was simple—if one person brought experience to the job, made twice the effort of those doing the minimum levels, and offered greater productivity, then it was equitable to pay him more. I will not claim that this system was easy to implement, but the employees appreciated the incentive, and the company benefited from it.

In general, employees fared far better when they hung on to their job and added value, rather than job-hopping for higher wages. The employee learned that hard work and added value would be recognized and rewarded. In the end, the company received exceptional effort. This approach put the employee and the company in a parallel position—and was more efficient and less expensive than the traditional system.

Trickle-Up Theory of Bonuses

Once LifeUSA became a publicly traded company, it was more difficult to use stock as a way to create parallel interests. In its place, a bonus plan was designed to accomplish the same objective.

Implementing this bonus system required us to cheat on a couple of established corporate compensation rules. Instead of starting at the top of the organization and allowing financial perks to (maybe) trickle down, the LifeUSA bonuses started at the bottom of the organization and worked their way to the top. Instead of the CEO being the first person to receive a bonus, he was awarded a bonus only after everyone else had received one. And, equally as important, the CEO bonus was a factor of the bonuses received by other employees.

The LifeUSA bonus plan was also unique in that it was not a single plan for the entire organization, but rather specific *niche* plans structured to the particular activity of each division. The standard corporate bonus plan was based on the company's achievement of certain sales, profits, or stock price levels. These may be effective measurements for the senior management of a company, but are not very effective for the vast majority of employees who find it difficult to measure their impact on the profits of an organization.

By isolating specific activities, that, when pooled together, created discernible value for the company, each division created their own *bonus pool*. At the end of the year, this bonus pool was distributed among all members of the division based on the value of their contribution.

Here is an example that illustrates this concept. When trying to build the securities division of LifeUSA, a bonus plan was designed to encourage and reward specific activities that ultimately would increase the value of the division. These were simple but concrete measurements that everyone could understand and effect—for every registered representative recruited to the company, $25 would go into the bonus pool. When a new representative produced the first piece of business, $50 was added to the bonus pool. For each $100,000 of business produced by a representative, $100 was put in the pool. These factors were then balanced with the control of expenses, so that if 1,000 representatives were recruited, but expenses exceeded budget, the bonus pool was reduced by a specific factor. By the same token, if the company experienced record recruiting activity, but expenses were below budget, the bonus pool was increased by another factor.

The idea behind this type of bonus is to communicate directly to employees that their activities are inextricably related to *enhancing the value* of the company and that their extra efforts benefit both the company and themselves *directly*. Everyone was able to relate to this parallel interest system of compensation.

With this program in place, when a potential representative called for information, he or she was never seen as a nuisance to the person taking the call, but rather as an *opportunity* to add to the bonus pool. With the potential to make money whenever new representatives submitted business or whenever an established representative wrote more business, employees were motivated to compete for that business.

The important point is that parallel interest plans such as these can be instituted in companies of any size. The critical element is that the plan be effectively communicated, fully understood, and structured so that employees feel they have direct power to influence results. Most important, the plan must be equitable. The principle of parallel interests rests on this principle of *sharing,* of creating win–win relationships with all the men and women your business touches.

Summary of the Secret

Sometimes the approaches outlined earlier are not available because the individual attempting to build an entrepreneurial culture is not high enough in the organization to implement financial incentives.

Let's say you are a department head and want to lead your group as an entrepreneur by developing parallel interests and shared values within the department. You may not be in a position to accomplish this through the use of financial rewards, but money is only one kind of incentive. There are many other ways you can reward employees. These other incentives have more to do with *psychic income* than cold hard cash.

Things like communicating openly, recognizing when a job is well done, offering clear evidence that you know who is adding value and who is not, developing a reputation for caring for the future of your employees even more than your own, and sharing the success of your department all become important when it comes to building the entrepreneurial culture of your department. Being able to recognize an employee who has added value to the company in front of others is often a payback more powerful than cash.

In the end, the entrepreneurial secret of parallel interests can come apart unless the organization implements specific equitable actions that prove to employees that there are tangible benefits to be gained by being in parallel.

11

Secret 9:
Be Constant,
Consistent,
and Concise

It's not what entrepreneurs do once in a while that makes them leaders, it's what they do all the time every time.

By definition, entrepreneurs are leaders. That's true no matter what size organization they may be running—be it a department, division, small business, or large corporation. Those who cannot lead others cannot be entrepreneurs. Fortunately, leadership is, for the most part, an acquired skill. Contrary to the old myth, leaders are not born, they are made.

Over the centuries, trying to identify and quantify the attributes of a leader has received almost as much attention as trying to distinguish the differences between men and women. (With just about equal success.) I have always been a student of leadership and leaders because understanding how leadership is developed and applied in real-life situations is a great laboratory for us to learn how to be leaders.

One thing I have discovered is that while leaders come in all shapes, sizes, personalities, and approaches, there are aspects of all leaders that are identical. The best part of this discovery is that these characteristics are something that all of us can learn, implement, and use to lead with.

I discovered that all leaders are constant, consistent, and concise in what they seek, say, and do. It sounds so simple, but these three Cs are essential and powerful elements of true leadership. In short, leaders not only "talk the talk," they "walk the walk."

This is a simple secret that entrepreneurs understand and it enhances their leadership ability. Bureaucrats, on the other hand, rarely see the need to be constant and consistent because employees are expected to follow rather than question the system. The concept of being concise is foreign to the bureaucrat's lexicon because they believe that an obfuscated issue increases their own importance.

The Test of Leadership

Entrepreneurs have an advantage over bureaucrats because they recognize that leadership is a "bad time" rather than a "good time" thing. What I mean is, anyone can lead when all the lights are green and the wind is at your back. In good times, the results of the organization often make it difficult to distinguish differences in leadership style between the bureaucrat and the entrepreneur. The entrepreneur is at his best when there is a challenge or crisis. The entrepreneur is stimulated by adversity and crisis. If things are too easy, the entrepreneur tends to be bored. It is in times of calamity that the entrepreneurial leader steps to the forefront with his constancy, consistency, and concise focus on the issue that gives followers comfort and direction. The rigidity of the bureaucratic style of leadership, on the other hand, stands up to crisis about as well as a haystack to a tornado. In times of upheaval, the entrepreneur becomes even more focused while bureaucrats run around like ants poked with a hot stick.

The difference between the crisis management style of entrepreneurs and bureaucrats is important because the question is not whether problems will surface, but when.

Entrepreneurial leaders—whether in established corporations or start-ups—are experts on Secret 9: They apply their leadership consistently, constantly, and concisely. In an entrepreneurial culture, there are no contradictions; there are no broken promises; there are no half-baked or shifting agendas. This approach positions the entrepreneurial culture to better tackle and overcome problems that do arise.

Without uniform application, the secrets of entrepreneurial leadership lose their value. Inconsistency breeds confusion, frustration, and even anger among employees. Eventually, turnover is higher and productivity sags. When managers send inconsistent messages to employees, the result is inconsistent performance, and a lack of faith, trust, and most of all, respect.

The members of an entrepreneurial culture are better prepared to work though problems because they learn to count on their leader being the same person day in and day out. At the same time, employees become unsteady and unsure when confronted with a quixotic bureaucratic environment marked by huge swings in the atmosphere—whether positive or negative. Employees expect consistency so that they clearly understand what is expected of them in any situation; they also thrive more productively when they get it.

Consistency across Management Styles

Through my 40-year career in business, I have worked for and with management supervisors of every stripe and hue. Interestingly enough, most management styles were anything but consistent. Many managers gave employees a fairly free hand in doing their jobs. Other supervisors were micromanagers who had a finger (sometimes a whole hand) in the day-to-day work of others.

Believe it or not, however, managers from either extreme or anything in between can be entrepreneurial in accomplishing goals. The key to their success is their consistency. Employees know what to expect from these managers. They always know where they stand. Management never, ever promises something they can't deliver. And even when things do not work out exactly as planned, they are first in line to get an explanation as to why, and how we can improve the situation. The result was that employees adjusted their approach accordingly and were never left in the dark about major employee issues.

Inconsistency Breeds Distrust

The greatest challenge we can experience as an employee is working for an inconsistent supervisor. Employees are very quick to note— and remember—when management practices what they preach and when they do not. They're just as quick to begin to ignore, or accept at face value (which is about the same), promises that are rescinded almost as soon as they are made.

Imagine being in a situation where employees are given instructions knowing those instructions could be changed unexpectedly and in opposition to the original instructions. It won't take long before this pattern of inconsistency leads to a breakdown of communications whereby employees don't know who or what to believe. This is a consistent style in bureaucratic cultures and recognized as the reason why so many such cultures are so inefficient.

What Is Consistency?

Consistency is not about having the staff meeting at the same time every week. It is not about using the same marketing strategy. It can be boiled down quite easily: *Say what you mean and mean what you say.*

Being an effective leader today requires accepting the fact that the mission is about the success of the organization, not personal aggrandizement. Leaders adopt the mission of the organization as the essence of their core beliefs and they refuse to be deterred from the mission no matter what happens. The job of the entrepreneur is to make sure his vision of the company is communicated consistently, concisely, and constantly with no trap doors and no hidden escape hatches. What you see is what you will *always* get.

Being Consistent Does Not Mean Being Inflexible

Entrepreneurial leaders are not only consistent in their behavior, but they are *passionate* about being consistent in what they do. Entrepreneurs may be flexible in adjusting to shifting conditions, but they do not easily change directions. They are not influenced by the nattering of outside influences, recognizing that there will always be those people who, for whatever reasons, will try to challenge, shake, and change the fortitude of a leader. Strong leaders may modify and adjust techniques, but the big picture remains consistent.

One of the chief benefits of this consistency is that those around the leader—employees, friends, family, even enemies—know they can rely on it. That is the essence of leadership. You *did* what you said you were going to do—again and again. People crave that type of consistency; that "stay-the-course" attitude in their leaders. Followers require a clearly defined image of what the leader is trying to provide before they will buy into that picture. If the leader is not willing to demonstrate a consistent, complete commitment to the objective, it is unrealistic to ask followers to give a full commitment to the leader.

The benefit of this approach was clearly brought home to me during the development of LifeUSA. We were fortunate to have very low turnover at the corporate offices but also among key field distribution leaders who joined the company in the early years.

The advantages of low employee turnover are obvious, but equally as important is retaining the loyalty of those in the field who sell the product. In the life insurance industry, independent field producers tend to move from company to company. (The same is true for the securities industry where stockbrokers and wholesalers tend to wander from company to company like nomadic tribesmen.) At LifeUSA, those who were leaders in production in the third year tended to be the same ones who led in the tenth year. This was not an accident, but the result of our leadership approach. These field leaders would often say to me, "Mac, you said what you were doing to do and you went out and did it and you are doing it today."

The moral of the story here is simple. Members of any organization look for consistency in their leaders. With it, they will tend to follow the leader anywhere, without it they will wander off looking for it.

Restless as a Willow in a Key West Hurricane . . .

The worst type of leader is one who is blown like a leaf in a hurricane. My criticism of many business leaders is that they are influenced by the last person to leave the office. Nothing is more bedeviling for employees than to have their team chief betray them with inconsistency. People want something to hang on to. They want something to focus on. They want to know they're on the right ship of fate, not some tramp steamer meandering toward the business shoals.

Historians believe that Jimmy Carter—despite his high intelligence and meticulous management style—will become a "forgotten" president because of his inability to remain focused and committed to a pronounced objective. No matter what the cause, as soon as resistance was encountered, Carter folded and moved to a newer vision.

Few would argue that Ronald Reagan was one of our brightest presidents. His idea of getting into the details was to be sure he knew what day it was, but he was clearly more effective than Carter and will be remembered well into history for his single-minded, focused battle to defeat the "evil empire."

Perhaps you remember when George H. W. Bush (the first one) stood before the Republican national convention in 1988 and promised, "Read my lips—No new taxes!" It was a defining moment in the campaign and may have won the election for Bush. But three years later, Bush agreed with the Democrats to raise taxes. Admittedly, valid arguments could have been made for the need to raise taxes, but that was not the issue. Despite Bush's high approval ratings from success in the first Gulf War, his retreat from what had been the cornerstone of his administration, cost him the credibility and confidence of the electorate. Certainly there were other reasons for Bush's loss to Clinton, but many political analysts cite this "change of direction" as an example of poor leadership and a key turning point in the election.

Keep It Simple, Stupid

The second prong of this secret is keeping things simple. In case you haven't noticed, traditional bureaucracies somehow believe that the issues that face a business are far too complicated for the average employee to understand. There seems to be a rule that the "little people" are great at operating, say, a punch press, but are too dull to understand real business problems and opportunities. This attitude is used by the bureaucrat to justify rigid process and procedure for everything that needs to be done.

This way of thinking may have been acceptable when people were uneducated, but it has no place in today's world. Yet, the idea hangs on, and employees are, thereby, disrespected.

Bureaucratic wannabe leaders prove they should be leaders by taking a simple issue and making it complicated. Bureaucratic leadership suggests that only the leader can understand the complexity of the issues and is therefore the only one who could lead. That's dumb and we ought to do away with that behavior together with the thinking that engendered it.

Effective leadership calls for a leader who can take truly complex issues and make them simple. Anyone can take a simple issue and make it complicated. (Just ask your IT guy how to turn on your computer!) It takes a talented leader to turn a complicated issue into a simple task. Demonstrate the ability to cut through the extraneous, identify the core issue and make it simple, and you have a talent that is fundamental to modern leadership.

Plans fail when tasks or objectives are perceived as too complicated. Paralysis sets in when people have a difficult time getting their minds around the problem, spotting the solution, and putting it into place. Good leaders know that the best way to overcome the obstacle of a complicated task is to identify simple things to do and help people do them.

Complicating the problem may appear to give the bureaucrat power; make him seem smarter and better than all the rest, but that is rarely the best way. The true entrepreneurial leader does just the opposite; he simplifies.

Just the Facts, Ma'am

Closely related to the issue of simplifying problems is the ability to cut through the complications and quickly get to the heart of the problem. Entrepreneurial leaders have an instinct to get to the core of the issue quickly and they don't fool around. There is no time for fooling around since it's a waste of everyone's time and energy.

Employees are looking for consistency in leadership style and expectations. And they want this consistency all the time—constantly. Consistency, conciseness, and constancy are what define entrepreneurial leaders. The ability to stay the course, stay on track, and maintain a solid vision forward demonstrates leadership confidence and control.

Putting Consistency to Work

How is it that in today's fast-paced, mile-a-minute business world a successful entrepreneur actually tends to become a more consistent leader?

First of all, he recognizes that not all things are going to be easy. He therefore disciplines himself to rise above daily business problems to provide leadership as consistently as possible. Yes, no doubt about it, that can be a major challenge. But when you think about it, I mean, really *think* about being consistent, it really isn't difficult at all. You simply do it.

Here are some thoughts:

- Say what you mean and mean what you say, consistently, concisely, and constantly. Remember, business is a marathon, not a 50-yard dash. It is rare that you won't be able to handle the problems that come with being an entrepreneur. And no matter how formidable the challenge, 10 years from now, it will seem like a tiny blip on the road to success.
- Establish a clear vision of your business and set distinct expectations. Make sure that you communicate that vision to your staff on a regular basis and keep them constantly informed.
- Never make promises that you cannot keep. At the end of the day, you might ask yourself how you could have been a more consistent leader today. If you find gaps in your consistency, make it a point to plug those chinks in your leadership fabric tomorrow. The key is *kaisen,* continual self-improvement.

Being consistent isn't always easy, nor is being concise and constant. Business pressures have a way of invading our life and leaving little room for the kind of behavior I'm prescribing. But it can be done.

Your responsibility as an entrepreneurial leader is not to single-handedly conquer the world. You will win no medals for working 80-hour weeks, putting out the most fires, or wielding the whip on your staff. Our job as an entrepreneur is to create the vision and motivate others to *continually* buy into that vision and make it their own. The secret to being a great leader is to get more out of those we lead—which in turn allows us to achieve our own maximum effort. And one of the keys to doing this is to be consistent, constant, and concise—every single day.

Summary of the Secret

The true entrepreneur internalizes Secret 9 and makes it core to his management arsenal: He applies leadership techniques that are— without fail—constant, consistent, and concise. In simple terms, the true entrepreneur talks the talk and walks the walk.

Without uniform management, leadership loses its value. Inconsistency breeds confusion, frustration, and even anger. The result is that employee morale suffers, productivity lags, and employee turnover rises. Is it any wonder that employees simply lose faith and trust in bureaucratic leadership?

The answer, of course, is to be consistent. Say what you mean and mean what you say. Speak your truth concisely, and avoid the urge to confuse or complicate. And, above all, establish a clear vision of your business's mission and communicate that mission to the troops as frequently as appropriate.

One final secret to effective entrepreneurial leadership: The true entrepreneur never promises more than he can deliver and always delivers more than he promises.

12

Secret 10: Treat Important People like Important People

People who are important to the success of an organization will strive for the success of the organization so long as they are treated as if they are important to the organization.

Remember the vastly popular sit-com *Cheers*? The show took place in a local Boston bar and was centered on an eclectic group of Bostonians (all Bostonians like to think they are eclectic) who always ended up coming back to this same bar. Why? Because they felt like they belonged: Everybody knows your name; everybody's glad you came. Having a sense of *belonging* made them feel welcome and appreciated.

Have you ever returned to a restaurant where the host greeted you by name, "Welcome back Mr. Johnson, so nice to see you again." Did that greeting make you feel important? Of course it did and I bet it made you want to come back to that restaurant again.

Has anyone you really respected ever come to you and asked your advice on something that was important to them? How did that make you feel? Were you complimented that someone you respected would think enough of you to ask your opinion about something? I bet you felt complimented; I know I would.

These examples are used to introduce you to a secret known to all entrepreneurs: *When an entrepreneur strives to make people feel welcome as a part of the group, appreciated for the value they bring, and respected for what they can contribute, then the members of the group feel wanted and important; in return, they will do anything to support his objectives.*

Entrepreneurs know that the secret to building an entrepreneurial culture is to motivate people to take an important role in the success of the company and the way to do that is to treat them as if their role was important to the success of the company. It is such a simple little thing, but entrepreneurs understand its power. If someone is important enough to determine your success or failure how would you treat them? Like someone who was important, right?

Avoid Bureaucratic Double-Talk

Bureaucratic organizations like to spout off about how important the employees are to the success of the company, even referring to employees as "associates" or "partners." Unfortunately, their actions do not back up their words. Bureaucratic managers do not believe that employees are a business's most important asset—they think *they* are. Bureaucrats get entirely too wrapped up in themselves and their P&L statements and forget that employees are the *key* to the financial success of any business. Entrepreneurs have a deep, honest belief that if a culture is to be successful, it must consist of a group of energetic, competent members who will go all out for the organization and the leader.

The secret to grooming such a team is to create the entrepreneurial environment that not only condones employee participation, but encourages it. In an entrepreneurial culture, all or nearly all employees are fully engaged.

Employees like these work with a passion and feel a profound sense of *connection* with their company. These are the employees who foster innovation and creativity in their work, and press hard to make it successful.

There are a number of ways that help foster the kind of participation that is essential to entrepreneurial success. These secrets are sprinkled throughout this book and are meant to help you create an inner philosophy of parallel thinking.

Include Your Staff in Decision Making

When a decision is to be made or a project to be initiated—especially something that could impact all employees—the best way to gain support from employees is to *always* engage them in the process. The entrepreneur understands that if people are given the opportunity to participate in and make a decision, they are more likely to take ownership of the selected course of action and promote the solution.

Besides, if those who are going to be doing the work are allowed to participate in the planning, they most likely have the needed experience to know what needs to be done. Moreover, if they are allowed to participate in the decision, there is a vested interest in seeing the action is successful.

Here is a simple example of what I mean. Let's say that rising costs require some changes in the company benefits package. The options are to raise premiums, copayments, deductibles, or reduce coverage. The entrepreneur does not really care what the solution is, just as long as costs are controlled. In this case, the entrepreneur goes to the employees to lay out the challenge and the options. He then asks them to come up with suggestions and make a recommendation as to what they feel is the best action regarding the benefits plan.

This is a small point, but it is part of the total process an entre-preneur employs when dealing with his people to demonstrate his respect for them, their input, and participation. When the change is made, not everyone may like the result, but they will be much more accepting because they participated in the decision. This approach reinforces another secret the entrepreneur has: *If you don't care what the decision is, let others make it.*

Entrepreneurial Cultures Are Not Necessarily Democratic

As I discuss the secret to making employees feel important and encour-aging participation in the process, don't make the mistake of think-ing that entrepreneurial cultures are democracies. They are not and shouldn't be. The leader still has to be the ultimate arbitrator of the decision, but the entrepreneur knows there is nothing to lose and a lot to gain by allowing others to participate.

Bureaucratic cultures are just the opposite. Managers and super-visors in a bureaucracy take the position that they know it all, and by sheer dint of their elevated positions, are inclined to believe they "know what's best" for all concerned. The general attitude is that asking others to participate in the decision process is a perceived sign of weakness. If changes need to be made to a benefits plan, they are announced, not discussed.

It's a dumb mistake. One of the things I learned early on as a CEO was the incredible depth of knowledge that most employees have about the business. I was continually amazed that they understood how things worked and what was needed to make things better. The entrepreneur encourages participation and is open to others who know more than he, while the bureaucrat is intimidated by the knowledge of others.

A good example of this bureaucratic know-it-all-attitude surfaced at a company where I was consulting. The chief marketing guy for the company approached me with a rather thorny problem. It seems his boss had ordered him to reduce the cost of the incentive plan for the salesforce by 7 percent. From his perspective, the problem was not cutting incentive compensation by 7 percent. That was easy—he could just do it. His concern was how to tell the salesforce that the cut had been made and get them to buy into it. Such a concern is typical in a bureaucratic culture where there is never a thought about inviting those impacted to participate in the decision.

I asked my worried bureaucrat one simple question: "Did he or his boss care how the cuts were implemented?" When he admitted that all he needed was 7 percent and didn't care where it came from, I asked him why not get the top salespeople to participate in the process. After all, the big hitters were going to be most affected so it would only be fair for them to participate.

Believe it or not, I thought that I actually saw the twinkle of an enlightened entrepreneurial thought pass through his mind. I thought for sure I had him when he queried, "Do you think they would actually do that?" This opened the door for me to say to him, "Why don't you go to these salespeople and explain to them what the problem is and offer them your thinking about ways to solve it. Then, ask them what they think could be done. Ask them what they would do if they were in your place. Get their thoughts and ideas."

I added that he didn't have to do what they recommended, but at least give them the opportunity to provide input. After all, it is possible that they could come up with a better solution, and in any event, they will have been given an opportunity to voice their opinion and participate in their destiny. Then when the decision is announced there is a better chance they will accept it.

He said, "Yeah, yeah, I will go talk to them." I went home that day proud of my accomplishment and with the hope that a budding entrepreneur had been uncovered.

So what happened?

Well, three weeks later, he unilaterally announced the new incentive plan at the annual sales conference. The only problem is that he never did go to the salespeople and ask for their ideas and participation. Clearly, they received the signal that they were not important enough to be included is these discussions that impacted their future. The company never did understand why sales began to fall, but at least the bureaucrats maintained their power and control to make the "right" decisions without interference from the "nonimportants."

Entrepreneurs recognize that employees desperately (and this is not hyperbole) want to participate in what is happening and they want to have an impact on your business's destiny. When we began the process of forming AIMS company for Allianz, a large number of people who had been at LifeUSA came to me looking to participate. Of all the reasons given for why they wanted to join the new venture, one stuck out the most. Over and over again they would say, "I just want to be involved again. I want to make a difference." They were not looking for money or titles, they just wanted to feel important and participate.

Most employees in bureaucracies feel that they have no impact on the organization. They feel like they don't really participate in what is happening. Therefore, they often lose interest and certainly their passion. They feel, quite rightly, that managers go off and make the decisions and then return from their Himalayan retreats and tell employees what's going to happen.

Employees don't like that. They want to participate. Employees on all levels like to feel that they are part of the team, and the team members are in parallel with one another, seeking the best result for all involved.

I'm sad to say that this is a classic example of a bureaucratic system rather than an entrepreneurial system. The solution that is finally acted upon may be the same, but in an entrepreneurial system the people feel they have participated. Even if their suggestions were not accepted, it makes it easier for them to go along with the system and foster that important entrepreneurial culture. That is what an entrepreneurial culture does. It takes the issues and allows people to participate.

Ask for Employee Input and Honestly Consider What They Tell You

Anybody who has run a business for any length of time knows that some employees are eager to air their viewpoints, but others are not. That's why entrepreneurial management is *proactive* in soliciting this input.

That means you've got to do more than hang a suggestion box in the employee break room. It means you regularly meet with your employees and—pointedly—ask for their views about issues that confront your organization. Questions are possibly one of the most powerful tools of a good leader. By not asking questions, you assume you know all the answers.

If asked, many employees will offer more than expected. This is particularly true if they are convinced that their suggestions are truly needed and that management can be trusted to consider their input.

What separates an entrepreneur from a bureaucrat is the willingness to listen and respond in a supportive, nonjudgmental way.

Employees will remain loyal and enthused only if the CEO and management demonstrate respect, integrity, honesty, and forthrightness through the process.

When you hold process improvement sessions, remember that *listening* is more important than talking. Keep your mouth shut and listen carefully. Then let the summary of data tell you what's happening.

An example of that kind of participation at LifeUSA was what we called the Shareholder Advisory Board (SAB). The board was made up of people in the field who would join us on an advisory counsel to management and learn what was happening in the company.

Actually, that's not so unusual. There are many companies who will bring in their salespeople and others to get their input. Sometimes, management just gives lip service to the idea, but others use the opportunity more creatively.

At LifeUSA, for example, we not only brought the field people in, we rotated home office people. There might be 10 field people on the SAB, and there would be 5 home office people, who participated. And that was terrific for the home office people. They got to answer a lot of questions the field reps didn't understand, and they got the same benefit.

The field reps would say, "Why can't you do this?" and the home office people would say, "Well here's why you can't do that and this is what the issue is."

By programming these meetings in this way, we built strong and trusting relationships. Both sides benefited. Both sides (or as many sides as you want to include) are allowed to participate. And you know what? The group often came up with some very creative and constructive ideas I would have never thought of.

The key is that in an entrepreneurial culture, people have a sense of *participating* in the company. They are not outsiders to the company. In a bureaucracy, everyone feels like an outsider. They feel like it's them against the system. It is the system against them. So they feel like outsiders. They don't feel as though their participation is welcome. And they certainly don't have a sense of ownership.

Be Transparent—Share Business Information

Employees feel connected to your business or your department when they are within the loop of corporate communication. We talk about that at length in another chapter, but for now, remember that successful leadership encourages strong communication systems between all employees. Moreover, sharing information with employees can generate reciprocal sharing whereby employees feel free to tell you what's going on in the company, including information you may know nothing about.

Listening generates both interest and motivation and is important to good leadership. Think about your own job. When your superiors don't listen to you, that spark of creative ingenuity is likely to be crushed. I mean, why bother to offer suggestions when nobody cares? On the other hand, when the boss pays attention to your need to make a difference, to make a real contribution to the business, you not only feel better about yourself, but about the importance of the job you've got. This is the secret that entrepreneurs know and believe in.

Hold Strategy Sessions

To identify changes needed to make your organization great, hold a strategy session. If a culture has been created that stresses the importance of the employees and they know that openness is encouraged and not squashed there is much to gain from these meetings. The key is for the leader of the area involved to lead the discussion and not take the bureaucratic approach of hiring a neutral facilitator to run the session. When the employees know their opinions are respected, they will feel free to give honest responses to such questions as:

- How are we doing as a business (department)?
- Do you think the company (our section) is on the right track?
- Does top management's strategy appear to be effective? How can it be improved?
- What needs fixing?
- What specific items stand in our way of becoming a better business?

Just one process improvement meeting can give you six months of things to fix in your organization. Using consensus, you can figure out what needs fixing first.

Recognize and Reward

One of the key premises of this book is that employees will perform above and beyond the call of duty when they have a stake in the result—when they participate in a process and are suitably rewarded for the value they add.

It's a simple truth: Employees will do more of whatever behavior leads to good things. Employees will contribute far beyond what you expect of them if their contributions are reinforced and rewarded.

As you will see elsewhere in this book, there are many ways to recognize, reward, and foster continued participation. Certainly, one way is *financial* rewards: bonuses, stock options, pay raises, and so on.

But sometimes as humans who happen to be employees, the best reward we can receive is the recognition of our effort and knowledge that someone appreciates our efforts. Entrepreneurs are masters at this approach and practice it often. Listening to what employees say, complimenting them as often as appropriate, publicly and privately acknowledging their contributions, and just patting them on the back for a job well done. It has to be deserved and sincere, but be careful not to dismiss this aspect of fostering participation. It may seem inconsequential, but it's certainly not unimportant to the employee to whom it is delivered.

Share the Value

There is another side of fostering participation and that is sharing in the value that has been developed and the value that the people have added. In a bureaucratic organization, people do not get to share in the value. If the business profit increases by 30 percent, the people who are most responsible for *causing* that increase ought to share in the added value. But ordinarily that's not the case. Usually, it's the CEO and his immediate underlings than rake in that corporate largesse. The little people, the folks who made it actually happen, are shut out.

When that happens, you don't create an entrepreneurial culture. You don't create a sense of ownership. You don't tie people to the organization, so the key in an entrepreneurial culture is to come up with a system that allows people to participate in the value. It is not always money that is the key part, but rather being able to participate in a system.

For example, Herb Kelleher, the iconoclastic CEO of Southwest Airlines, created a corporate culture that made Southwest employees well known for taking themselves lightly but their jobs seriously. I remember reading that Kelleher was being honored on Wall Street for the accomplishments of Southwest. There were, I'm told, about 10 or 12 people from the airline who were there with him at this big affair. And who were they? There were baggage handlers, flight attendants, pilots, ticket agents, and other rank and file. There were no senior guys there.

These people were participating in this high-level meeting. That is a great example of how it is possible to build an entrepreneurial culture by allowing the people to participate in everything that goes on about the company.

Your Ship Has Arrived

At LifeUSA, we once told the agents that if they wrote a billion dollars worth of business, we would charter a boat and take them on a cruise in the Caribbean. That was a neat deal and the kind of powerful incentive that was great for the company and its agents.

But what about all of the home office employees who would be left out? Well, we told them we couldn't take the entire home office, but we did set up a system that allowed a large number of people from the home office to go on this cruise.

If the employee could earn, say, "owner of the month" or "owner of the year" (independent awards open to all LifeUSA employees), his or her name would be added to the pot and at the end of the year, we'd select the top winners. We did the same thing for departments that achieved a certain level of activity. They could add names into the hat.

We ended up taking 250 agents and 100 or 125 home office employees. It was terrific. What the program created was a sense of participation in the awards program. In the end, it was a fair and equitable way to get everybody—from the mailroom on up—to focus on and participate in this billion dollar bash. They weren't just there processing, they were participating.

We did the same kind of companywide reward system for another big event. Shortly after Allianz merged with LifeUSA, we decided to sponsor a golf tournament that was to be held in Des Moines, Iowa.

Now, when bureaucratic companies do this sort of thing, off goes the chief executives, their senior people, and their big customers. They're flown first-class to the tournament site where they are wined and dined.

That's a position we did not want to take. We wanted to foster the entrepreneurial management lifestyle of LifeUSA in our new Allianz working environment. And we wanted to say to those people working in the home office that *you* are as important as our customers and our chief executives.

One of things we did was set up ways for people who worked in the home office to get to Des Moines to participate in that golf tournament. We set up a series of buses so that everybody could go on certain days. Because the tournament ran a whole week, we would run buses down there and party along the way. When our employees arrived, they'd get the VIP treatment, including meeting the top players, and even caddy for them if they wanted to.

The whole purpose was to make these employees feel that they truly were our real VIPs. We wanted to communicate that they were important to us.

In later years, after I left the company, the busses stopped running, the event was moved to Florida, and the home office employees got the shaft. They're sitting in their cubicles, hearing about how all the executives escaped from the subzero February cold in

Minnesota to enjoy the balmy sunshine on a tournament golf course in Boca Raton. Now is that building an entrepreneurial culture or is that allowing bureaucracy to take over?

Always Keep Commitments and Promises

There is no better way to destroy trust and a sense of participation than by breaking promises you've made to employees. This is particularly true when it's done habitually. Keeping your word is paramount to building trust and employee participation. The simple secret to building this support is to say what you mean and mean what you say. And when you do that consistently, employees will understand that commitments are never taken lightly, and promises are always kept.

Summary of the Secret

The entrepreneur knows the ultimate secret to the success of the organization. Recognizing the importance of employees to business success and showing that you believe this by the way you interact with employees. Things like:

- Be entirely transparent with your employees.
- Invite employee participation in your business decisions.
- Provide abundant opportunities for your employees to grow and utilize the full range of their many talents.
- Adopt wages, pay scales, bonuses, and profit-sharing methodologies that reward employees for superior performances.
- Engage the employee with ongoing communication and provide feedback on job performance—particularly business performance and its needs and opportunities.

- Always keep your commitments and promises.
- Rub shoulders with your employees; meet and greet.
- Establish opportunities for employee rewards and recognition for outstanding contributions.

The secret of fostering entrepreneurial participation in the culture is to actively and sincerely invite members into the circle of control. That means talking to them, inviting their suggestions, taking a risk on their ideas, and accepting the occasional failure that always accompanies creativity, no matter the source.

Management should abandon the command-and-control business model that seems to be embedded in the DNA of bureaucracies. Businesses have to trust their employees and, as I've noted more fully in another chapter, share corporate wealth more equitably.

All you need to do is tap into the incredible treasure trove of knowledge your employees hold. Then harness their energies and channel their efforts to help your organization become great.

13

Secret 11: Do Simple Things—But Simply Do Them

Anyone can make simple things complicated.
The talent is in making complicated things simple.

If forced to use one word to describe one specific aspect of every real entrepreneur, that word would be *simple*. Asked for the same regarding a bureaucrat and the word would be *complicated*.

These two approaches to management are so divergent in approach and outcome that, like the ever-expanding universe, they cause entrepreneurial and bureaucratic cultures to grow more and more dissimilar.

If running the gauntlet was a right of passage for males in some primitive cultures, then taking something very simple and making it very complicated is the right of passage for bureaucrats. The funny thing is that it takes more time to continually make everything complicated, but bureaucrats, like prisoners serving a life sentence, have nothing but time. Entrepreneurs, on the other hand, seem to opt for the simple approach because they don't have time to fool around.

It was a nice (if frustrating) compliment when, after LifeUSA became a clear winner, people would suggest how easy and simple it was for the company to achieve success. For them, looking back at the development of LifeUSA success, it seemed obvious that what we did was simple and (most aggravating) something that anyone could have accomplished. Of course, they were right on all counts, but many of them were the same people who had pooh-poohed the idea of LifeUSA at the start.

The basis for the success of LifeUSA, as with any successful entrepreneurial culture, was to *do simple things but simply do them.* Ask any former LifeUSA owner today the reason for the success of the company and they will repeat that mantra.

Unfortunately, the story is just the opposite for bureaucratic cultures. In fact, bureaucratic organizations are identified and defined by the complexity of their structure and operations. Entrepreneurs know the secret to beating the system is to simply keep it simple!

Complicated versus Simple

Let me set the stage in order to explain what I mean when I say entrepreneurs do simple things but simply do them. Let's use customer service as an example.

Business consultants (the Grand Masters of complexity) make a living (more like a fortune) counseling companies on the process and techniques of providing quality customer service. They enlist research, focus groups, matrix studies, customer mining, and a whole bunch of other poppycock all designed to create a plan for "customer focus." I remember sitting (sleeping really) through a 296-slide PowerPoint presentation by a consultant who had been hired by a large Canadian bank to help them figure out how to provide good customer service. The graphs and charts were mind numbing. (I can't imagine how much money was wasted on this effort.) Once the consultants have finished, then the internal implementation plans and meetings begin. More time and money wasted.

Along this line, a couple of years ago, I was asked to participate on a customer focus task force for a large international organization that owned over 100 different companies in every part of the world. Even though these companies operated in different markets and diverse cultures, in the end the company (like all good bureaucracies) decided to define and delineate customer service at the holding company level and drive those results down through the organization. (In my defense, it should be pointed out that after about three or four task force meetings I was "disinvited" off the task force. For some reason, they were tired of me telling them how wasteful, bureaucratic, and futile their efforts were.)

Certainly, at LifeUSA we wanted to provide good customer service. In fact, it was one of our most important objectives for differentiating this upstart company from the established competition. At LifeUSA, our customers were the agents who sold the product. (The policyholders were the customers of the agents.) Without the help of outside consultants (no way we could have afforded their outlandish fees), we tried to tackle the idea of good customer focus. And what did we come up with? LifeUSA defined good customer service by what we called a "48-hour challenge." Once the agent had submitted all the application paperwork to LifeUSA, we promised to issue the new policy in 48 hours or we'd pay the agent $100. This may not seem like a big thing, but it was. Industry standards for issuing policies at the time was more like 48 days, so the promise of 48 hours was quite a differentiating point from the competition. Few companies are willing to really back up the promise of good service, but LifeUSA did by promising the payment of $100 if we failed to deliver.

Was the task of issuing a policy in 48 hours complicated? Yes. How was it made simple so the promise could be kept? Each part of the process was broken down to simple steps, but steps that were simple to do. And, then we did them.

Sure, some would suggest that it was easy for a new company, with not much business, to offer this service, but very difficult for the larger established companies. Not true. LifeUSA was still promising the 48-hour service 15 years later when receiving 5,000 applications a week, just as it had when receiving 50 applications a week. (There were many LifeUSA innovations copied by other companies, but none ever tried to match the 48-hour challenge.)

What's the point here? Well, for one, it shows that it is possible to take a very complicated process such as customer service and break it down to its simplest components. Bureaucrats believe complicated problems call for complicated solutions. Entrepreneurs don't have time for complicated solutions so they seek simple ones. After all that the agent had to go through to make the sale, the most important thing to him was to get the policy issued as quickly as possible.

The idea of a 48-hour challenge was to find and implement a very simple way to communicate the standards of good service to all parties. The LifeUSA employees knew exactly what the standards for good customer service were and the customers (the agents) knew what to expect. From a management perspective, the results of the 48-hour challenge was a simple way to measure the quality of service being provided. Each month, by measuring the number of times the $100 had to be paid by the number of applications received management had a clear picture of the quality of service being provided.

That brings me to another example of how the entrepreneur looks for simplicity while the bureaucrat looks for complexity. A consistency with any large bureaucratic culture is a plethora of management reports. Sometimes it seems the largest department in a bureaucratic company is the one that collects, collates, analyzes, and distributes management reports. No one escapes the pain as each department and division must prepare and submit these reports to the "planning department." The bureaucrats then use these reports to "manage" the company. Of course, they need these reports because very few bureaucrats are hands-on enough with the company to actually know what is happening. You've been there and I'm sure you know exactly what I mean about these management reports. And you know what a waste of time and money they are.

It's not that performance information is unimportant; rather the entrepreneur takes a simpler approach. That's because the entrepreneur knows a simple little secret to judging the performance of the company. The secret the entrepreneur knows is: *If each month, quarter, or year the company performance gets better than it was before, then the company will do better.* How simple is that?

I have been CEO of some pretty large companies. The assets, sales, and revenues of these companies would run into the billions of dollars. And yet at the end of each month, quarter, and year, the only management report (provided on no more than two pages) I wanted showed me the performance of the company relative to what we had done in the past. (Another reason may have been that I didn't want to admit that I was not smart enough to understand all the fancy reports.)

Here's what I wanted to know: What were the average sales per employee? What were the average numbers of applications per employee? How many new agents were recruited? What percent of contracted agents were actually writing business? How many 48-hour challenges were paid? What was the ratio of total expenses to total employees?

There were a few other categories, but I think you get the point. I knew that if these ratios were improving, then the company was growing and performing well, and all the rest would take care of itself. The detailed financial reports were necessary and important, but I used those reports to validate what I already knew, not to run the company.

One of the most often heard complaints from our staff after Allianz acquired LifeUSA was the geometric increase in management reports that had to be developed and sent to the bureaucrats in Germany. Of course, this was to be expected because the staff bureaucrats at Allianz needed something to do and the executives tried to use the reports to manage the company.

The concept of simplicity over complexity is not just relegated to operational plans and management reports. Simplicity is what makes an entrepreneurial culture possible. Simplicity should be pervasive in all elements of the organization.

Training programs, product development, communication, compensation systems, and incentive programs all lend themselves to falling into the trap of complexity. They are heaven-sent gifts for the bureaucrat. The entrepreneur recognizes that allowing issues like these and others to slip into complexity can clog and hinder the performance of the entire organization.

As an example, I would give a prize to anyone other than the most sophisticated bureaucrat who could explain some of the incentive compensation plans in place at large bureaucracies. You know what I mean. I'm sure you've seen them or even been a participant. These plans (developed by bureaucrats) get so complicated there is no way they can be understood, let alone provide incentive. The entrepreneur does not countenance this approach and is constantly fighting for simplicity.

Having experienced it firsthand, I'll be the first to admit that as an organization grows, greater complexity is inevitable, but just because the issues and challenges are more complex does not mean the solutions have to be. Certainly human resource department procedures have to change when a company grows from 5 to 500 or 5,000 employees, but the same *attitude* of doing simple things but simply doing them, still works.

I am confident in the voracity of this belief because that is what enabled LifeUSA to continue the 48-hour challenge when the number of weekly applications increased from 50 to 5,000 and because the 500th employee was treated the same way as the 5th employee.

Sure, it takes commitment and effort to keep things simple as an organization grows, but that's the difference between an entrepreneur and a bureaucrat; and that's the difference that keeps an entrepreneurial culture from becoming a bureaucracy.

Summary of the Secret

This is one of the most important secrets an entrepreneur can use to beat the system, yet this is one of the shortest chapters in the book. But that is the beauty of this secret. I hate to give lawyers credit for anything, but entrepreneurs can learn a secret from them in the way they go about parsing complicated cases.

The good lawyers (both of them) approach a complicated case by attempting to identify the core issues that will ultimately determine the outcome of the case and ignore the superfluous claims.

The true entrepreneur takes the same approach when facing business issues. Where the bureaucrat looks at every possible issue and gives them equal weight, the entrepreneur steps back and focuses only on the most critical. He asks the question: What is important here and what is not? Once the issues have been singled out it becomes much easier to find simple solutions. In the end, the entrepreneur beats the system by identifying simple things to do and encourages his people to simply do them.

Most bureaucrats are pros at making things more complicated than they need be. It's like they're all graduates of that school that teaches how to write the assembly instructions for that chaise lounge you bought at Ikea. They appear to go out of their way to make life complicated for everybody.

Plans fail when tasks or objectives are perceived as too complicated. Paralysis sets in when people have a difficult time getting their minds around the problem, spotting the solution, and putting it into place. Making the problem more confusing, more difficult, may appear to give the bureaucrat more power; they think it may make them seem smarter, or better than all the rest. But it's never the best way. The true entrepreneur does just the opposite. He doesn't try to prove his imperial genius or justify his six-figure salary by making things more complicated. Instead, he proves what a great leader he is by making complicated things simple.

14

Building from the Inside Out: Lessons Learned in Creating AIMS

The intensity of bureaucratic resistance is in inverse proportion to that which would benefit the organization the most.

The previous chapters of this book have outlined and defined what I believe are the secrets to achieving success and reaping the benefits of being an entrepreneur. As you can see, I view entrepreneurialism in the broad context of a lifestyle, rather than the generally accepted narrow sense of "being in business for oneself." As we have learned, the true entrepreneur is not really in business for himself, but rather works for the benefit of others—both individuals and organizations. In so doing, the true entrepreneur achieves much more in the way of personal accomplishment, reward and satisfaction than would be possible when working only for individual, self-centered goals.

A central thesis of this book is that it is possible to be an entrepreneur and build an entrepreneurial culture within the confines of a larger, well-established bureaucratic organization. This includes behaving as an entrepreneur no matter what your job may be. It is possible to manage yourself, a department, or even the division of a company in an entrepreneurial way.

But I have an even larger question: *Is it possible to actually build an entrepreneurial company within a much larger bureaucratic organization?*

From my personal perspective and experience the answer is yes, but it is difficult and frustrating. I know this for a fact, because after five years of comfortable retirement on the beach in Key West, Allianz SE of Munich Germany, one of the largest (and most bureaucratic) organizations in the world, asked me to come back to work as a consultant. Allianz wanted me to take a lead role in a major international initiative to position Allianz as a leader in offering financial products designed to provide income during retirement.

My prerequisites for involvement were fairly simple (from my perspective), but I recognized that Allianz would find them difficult to accept. What I wanted more than anything was to build this new company on purely entrepreneurial concepts.

In addition, instead of working as part of an existing Allianz company, I demanded the company be completely independent of Allianz. Further, I wanted it to be built from scratch as a start-up operation. Much to my surprise, these conditions were quickly accepted. But, as they say, the devil is in the details.

The Burgeoning Retirement Market

To be honest, I did not see much of a challenge in the assignment. After all, in financial services the "retirement market" is the growth opportunity of the century. During the next 30 years, over 60 million American Baby Boomers will reach retirement age. Collectively, this group has access to an estimated $20 trillion dollars in personal wealth. Any financial institution—bank, investment firm, or insurance company—that could be successful in meeting the retirement needs of the Baby Boomers would be the big winners.

Even though this was to be a start-up effort, financial resources would not be a problem. After all, Allianz is one of the world's largest companies. In addition, Allianz had been excited by the success of their acquisition of LifeUSA and had asked me to conduct numerous meetings and seminars aimed at implanting entrepreneurial attitudes and skills in bureaucratic cultures. My attitude was that all the pieces were in place for swift, dramatic success and, compared to starting LifeUSA, this was going to be a piece of cake. Little did I know!

I soon discovered that it would have been easier to start 100 new LifeUSAs compared to the difficulty of starting an entrepreneurial company within the bowels of a bureaucratic organization such as Allianz.

To be fair, there are very few bureaucratic organizations that would ever allow this type of initiative to see the light of day, let alone a monolith like Allianz with over 170,000 employees, operating in 70 countries, managing in excess of $1.5 trillion of assets and possessing a record of international success that is envied by many. The worldwide leader of Allianz, Michael Diekmann, is to be given real credit for supporting and allowing the effort to move forward. Of course, that did not mean creating this new entrepreneurial business would be easy.

Despite professed desires, lip service, and protestations to the contrary, Allianz could easily be the poster child for the bureaucratic society. Not only did the Allianz bureaucratic culture demonstrate high proficiency in the ability to do nothing, at least half the people involved (including members of the board of management) worked to see the project stillborn. Every tried and true proven roadblock available was thrown in the path of the birth and development of the project. (For purposes of reference as we move forward in this chapter, the name of the new company Allianz Income Management Services, is referred to as AIMS.)

This was not the first time I had done battle within a bureaucratic organization, but it was my first time to take on and challenge the very core of the beast. What I failed to recognize—and should have— going in was that the foundation of this effort—a new entrepreneurial company—was an anathema to the very core of the Allianz business model, which was anything but entrepreneurial. This presented a unique situation because the very birth mother of the concept— Allianz—worked to stunt the baby's growth, if not suffocate it. Talk about the idea of animals "eating their young!" As a result of this experience, I would argue that if an entrepreneurial culture can sprout within a company such as Allianz, it can be grown anywhere.

In the process of building this company, I have learned some simple secrets that will make it much easier for you to succeed in building an entrepreneurial group within a bureaucratic organization.

Call them bonus secrets if you will, and add them to your toolkit:

1. Recognize the business model of the organization you are working with. Understand you are not going to change it. Look for a way to beat the system without attacking it.
2. Seek approval for your project at the highest possible level.

3. Have an unshakable commitment to the basic inviolate principles of your effort.
4. If you have received approval as to the general concept, be willing to move forward prior to formal sign off on the details.
5. Make the bureaucrats play from and respond to your game plan.
6. Work to entwine the organization in your efforts so that it becomes impossible for the bureaucrats to stop you.
7. Never forget that bureaucrats never give up.

Let's use some of my experiences with Allianz to review how these simple secrets can help you beat the system. As you read these bonus secrets, it may be helpful for you to think about how they apply to your business.

Bonus Secret 1: Recognize the Business Model of the Organization You Are Working With

It is difficult for an entrepreneurial culture to develop and flourish within a large bureaucratic organization because of the bureaucracy's slavish passion to protect an embedded business model and the fundamental philosophy of a bureaucracy to centralize control and consolidate power.

Bureaucrats have a vested interest in the status quo. The bureaucrat exists to protect "what it is," not seek out "what it could be." Bureaucrats realize there is no need for them in an entrepreneurial culture. Let's face it: an organization would not have grown large enough to be bureaucratic if its business model had not been a success.

The problem is that as a company becomes successful, the budding bureaucracy causes the business model to become rigid and resistant to any type of modification. Regardless of any changes to the environment in which the company operates, the "we've always done it that way" mantra begins to hold sway. As a result, any whiff of change causes bureaucratic nostrils to flare.

By its nature, the bureaucratic organization focuses on what it has already acquired and is protecting its turf. From the perspective of the bureaucratic organization, the entrepreneurial inclination for diversity, flexibility, adjustment, and sharing of value is considered the enemy.

Allianz is the epitome of this reality. It was difficult enough for the bureaucrats to accept the AIMS concept of entrepreneurialism, but the problem was compounded by the business model of the new company that was in direct conflict with the accepted business plan of Allianz.

Acquire and Control Business Model

The Allianz business model is based on the idea of "acquire and control." Such a model translates into the belief that the only way to grow is to *acquire* the growth by buying other companies. Once you've bought the company, it's a simple matter to fold it into your operation and lop off the excess employees as though you were trimming a piecrust.

It is difficult to criticize a company such as Allianz that has followed this model to become the 12th largest corporation in the world. However, in a changing world, the inherent inflexibility of this approach can lead to problems. What if there is an attractive market to be entered, but there are no companies to acquire? What if the acquisition price for entry into a market becomes too expensive to be practicable? The bureaucratic organization is left with few alternatives. This can lead to foolish mistakes and failure, all because of bureaucratic enslavement to an outmoded business model. (Sears and IBM come to mind here.)

Control is another pillar of the Allianz business model. The bureaucracy adopts the attitude of, "We bought this company with our money and we deserve the right to say how it should be run and reap any and all the benefits." *Share* is not a word in the bureaucratic dictionary. A key tenet to the business model of the new company was that value created was to be shared with those directly involved with creating the value.

I bring up this background to demonstrate how alien the entrepreneurial philosophy of AIMS is from the Allianz acquire-and-control model. Not only is this approach in direct conflict with the "proven" Allianz acquire-and-control model, but it is also perceived as a threat. If the venture is successful, then possibly other Allianz companies will want to adopt a similar business model and that will require a change in the status quo of the Allianz system. We all know that bureaucrats view change as the number one threat to their power.

The fact is that you can't change this type of system so you have to find a way to beat the system.

Working Outside the Box

The secret to beating the system when your efforts are in conflict with an embedded business plan is to get as far outside the business model as possible while still allowing the bureaucrats to believe the ultimate result and control rests in their power.

This may sound conflicting—if not confusing mumbo-jumbo—but in reality, it can be simple.

AIMS was formed as a ground-zero start-up, which was a huge advantage. Allianz bureaucrats had no experience in creating an SOP of rules to straitjacket an entrepreneurial culture. The bureaucrat always wants to tread on a known path and will seldom stray from it. Clearly, AIMS was a new path for Allianz. As a start-up, there was nothing for the bureaucratic sticky fingers to control.

In addition, despite the fact that Allianz initially owned all of the stock, AIMS was considered an independent company. Yes, it was owned by Allianz, but it wasn't viewed as an "Allianz company" since it had not been acquired. As part of this fiction, AIMS is not listed as an Allianz subsidiary and employees of AIMS are not considered employees of Allianz. Because of this independence, the bureaucrats were encouraged to rationalize the venture as more akin to a stock investment. I know the logic is stupid, but sometimes the best way to deal with stupid rules is to apply stupid logic.

So if AIMS was moved outside the business model, how did we appease the power-and-control bureaucrats? We gave them three perks:

1. Allianz had the right to name a majority of the board of directors.
2. Even though employees and agents would own shares in the value of AIMS, only Allianz stock had voting powers.
3. Allianz had the ultimate guaranteed right to "acquire" the company by "calling" the stock of all other shareholders at an agreed price.

This structure allowed the bureaucrats of Allianz to believe (or at least rationalize) that AIMS was within the business model while allowing those of us in the AIMS organization the freedom to build an entrepreneurial culture. We didn't change the system, but we did beat it. And that's a secret you can use profitably when you know the business model you're up against.

Bonus Secret 2: Seek Approval for Your Project at the Highest Possible Level

This is a simple and seemingly obvious secret, but it is amazing how many people attempt to battle the bureaucracy of an organization single-handedly.

In my book *Cheat to Win,* I shared my strategy for gaining the approval of the Hartford CEO for the ITT Life marketing campaign that enabled us to move forward with confidence as we battled the bureaucracy. Quite simply, our strategy was "act now, ask questions later." In the AIMS situation, I knew from past experience that Michael Diekmann, the CEO of Allianz believed in the benefits of an entrepreneurial culture and that he was, in general, supportive of our efforts.

Neither one of these approvals cleared the path for our actions, but they did give us an important leg up to fight the good fight with the bureaucrats.

As a practical matter, not everyone seeking approval for an initiative that challenges the bureaucracy of an organization has access to the very top. And I wouldn't suggest that, in an effort to employ this secret, you try to circumvent the management channels in an organization.

The reality is that the impact of your project will be fairly close to your experience and job level. In the personal examples offered here, I was already at or near the top of the organization so it was natural for me to have access to high levels within the organization. But even so, I worked my way through the channels to the very top.

As a younger agency manager or department head, my entrepreneurial projects did not touch the core of the organization (only my direct areas of responsibility), so approval was sought from levels above me.

Knowing the Big Picture

When seeking approval from higher-ups, understand that what you seek is endorsement for the *concept,* not the details of your project. Keep those to yourself. Agreement from the "bigwigs" (at least bigger wigs than you are) on the big picture is all the license you need to battle bureaucrats over the details.

Yet, no matter where you are in an organization, the fundamentals of the bureaucracy actually make it easier for you to gain approval at higher levels than you might expect. No bureaucrat wants to make decisions because decision making confers *responsibility* for your actions. Accountability is the last thing a smart bureaucrat wants or needs.

When I was CEO of ITT Life, my boss agreed with my marketing concept, but did not want to have his fingerprints on the project, so he passed me up to his boss and so on until I actually reached the very top of Hartford Insurance. The same was true at Allianz. The people in charge of North America liked the concept of the retirement market, but wanted to be able to "share the blame" if things did not work out. As a result, both the international CEO and the board of management became "implicated" in the plot. With such high level involvement, the bureaucrats below were weakened.

For any chance of success with an entrepreneurial project, you must sell the concept as far up the chain as possible. Of course, you run the risk of reaching a level that outright rejects the idea. If that happens and you continue forward, there is little likelihood of success because you will be running naked through the gauntlet of bureaucrats. However, moving up the chain for approval is worth the risk and there may not be much risk anyway.

The higher up the chain you go, the less time and involvement that person gives to your project. The hierarchy of a bureaucratic organization always assumes those below have worked through the details so that they don't have to. This also allows them to blame the people below if something goes wrong.

All this leads to the validity of the simple secret that the higher the level of approval for your project, the stronger you will be at fighting off the bureaucrats.

Bonus Secret 3: Have a Firm Commitment and Understanding about the Basic Inviolate Principles of Your Effort

With AIMS, our principles were simple:

- To be an independent company outside the direct control of the bureaucrats
- To be an entrepreneurial culture founded on the concept of sharing the risk and value built

Once these principles were established, we were willing to give the bureaucrats anything they wanted, so long as they did not impinge on these principles. It's like buying a car. Once you've made the agreement you allow your spouse to pick out the color and the options.

The key is to let the bureaucrats win all the battles, while you win the war. Be willing to accept any structure or form, just so long as your basic principles are not violated. To do this, be willing to stand your ground and even abandon the project if the core principles are breached.

There is an interesting psychology that comes into play in these situations. The fact is that most business bureaucrats (as opposed to government bureaucrats) have a silent respect and admiration for those who are the doers—the entrepreneurs—in an organization. They don't understand how a doer does what he does and they could not do it themselves, but honest bureaucrats have an inherent understanding that it must be done—if only for the reason that someone doing something creates work for the bureaucrat to do. Confusing logic? Well, that's the bureaucracy.

Knowing this dynamic allows you to "draw a line in the sand" with the bureaucrats regarding your project. Trust me, bureaucrats will never challenge you on principle—only on process. This does not mean they won't come at you from different angles to probe and test you, but once they know where your line has been drawn, they will respect it. But you need the strength of your commitment.

Bonus Secret 4: Once You Have Received Approval of the General Concept, Be Willing to Move Forward without Agreement on the Details

If you live in a bureaucratic world, you will *never ever* receive final sign off on the details, so don't waste precious time waiting.

In earlier years as I tried to shift ITT Life into an entrepreneurial mode, we literally took the bull by the horns. Once we had approval for our marketing campaign, we independently moved forward setting strategy, developing plans, and taking action to implement the initiative. In fact, we established a 100-day launch program and by the time the bureaucrats came calling, the train had left the station and there was little they could do to stop it.

The same situation occurred at AIMS. Once general approval had been granted from on high, even though we had only a verbal authorization, we moved forward. The important point is that we moved forward on the basis of an implied assumption that the company would be structured as we had recommended.

Even before the company had been incorporated, we began recruiting people to join the effort, looking for office space and leasing office furniture. Early on, we had offices up and running and people working hard building the processes and procedures to run the company.

You know the old saying about keeping one step ahead of the law? Well, if you are to be successful fighting bureaucrats, the same logic needs to be applied. You have to constantly keep one step ahead of the bureaucrats. If you let the bureaucrats catch up or get ahead of you, they will build roadblocks. If you keep them in your dust, all they can do is shake their fists at you.

Adopt the Motto: Be Prepared

There is an important caveat here. With general approval in your pocket, it is okay to move forward without bureaucratic approval, but you better "have your knitting together" and know exactly what you are doing. The only way to stay one step ahead of the bureaucrats is to make sure you don't trip over your own actions. Trip up and they will trample you. This takes us back to a discussion earlier in the book when we established that a key to beating the system is to have intimate knowledge of the system.

In the case of AIMS and the office space (and all the other actions taken), our previous experience and knowledge of Allianz process and procedures allowed us to comply with requirements without prior approval. For example, we hired a law firm that had previously negotiated leases for Allianz. They knew what Allianz required in property leases. When the bureaucrats came calling about the office leases, there was nothing for them to complain about, except that we had not come to them first. (Shame, shame!)

Working under the shield of "implied consent" allows you to overcome one of the most frustrating constraints of a bureaucracy: the inability to make a decision and move forward on even small issues.

Bonus Secret 5: Make the Bureaucrats Play from and Respond to Your Game Plan

In simple terms, never get in a planning (or pissing) session with bureaucrats. Remember, your objectives and those of a bureaucrat are in direct conflict. As an entrepreneur, you want to get something done ("Whip it! Whip it Good!"), while the bureaucrat wants to do nothing.

The only way to resolve this conflict is to present the bureaucrat with a plan and what appears to be various options. And if you have done it right, whatever they pick you can live with because you selected the choices.

When attempting to build an entrepreneurial company within a larger bureaucratic organization, you will never be able to elicit specific help from the bureaucrats simply because their nature prohibits such activity and they have no experience on which to draw. (This latter point really helps when you are doing battle with them.)

Bureaucrats are much happier and actually helpful when you lay out specific plans and offer them the right to be involved. As a way of demonstrating just that point, I drafted a comprehensive memo on the subject and sent it to the Allianz bureaucracy in April 2006. We spent the balance of the year fighting with the bureaucracy as they tried to chew up our plan. All the while, we were moving forward with the company. The memo was important enough to be included in the Appendix, although it was a bit too long to include here.

This memo served as the basis for discussion and allowed us to define the debate. The important point is that the bureaucratic debate over AIMS was confined to the items discussed in this memo. We controlled the playing field. This forced the bureaucrats to focus on the issues we defined and avoided the potential of us being led astray.

For almost a year, the debate centered on this memo as the bureaucrats responded to our plan—not theirs! This approach allowed us to be true to our principles of specific focus, independence, and sharing while allowing the bureaucrats to feel as though they actually impacted the plan. The fact is they impacted the "margins" of the plan but not the plan itself.

Much of the debate was not over whether AIMS was independent, but what form the independence would take. We did not care what form the independence took, just so long as we were independent. The debate centered not on whether AIMS would share value with those who created value, but what form that value sharing would take. We did not care what form the value sharing took, just so long as the value sharing was in parallel with the value received by Allianz.

In the end, AIMS emerged as an independent marketing/administrator company owned by Allianz of America but creating, developing, issuing, and servicing policies for Allianz Life. (Ironically, even as Allianz Life and Fireman's Fund Insurance Company have lost much of their independence due to an, at best, misguided bureaucratic effort at synergy and consolidation, AIMS was shielded from that activity.)

Power and control are always more important to a bureaucrat than to an entrepreneur. The end objective for the bureaucrat is control, while the objective of the entrepreneur is ownership of shared value. In the case of AIMS, there was no need for control on the part of the employees and agents, so both sides achieved what they wanted.

The Bureaucratic Shuffle

All during the year of dialogue (and I am being nice to call it that), the bureaucrats huffed and puffed, postured and protested, fought and flailed over the details of the AIMS structure. Every time they came close to threatening the basic entrepreneurial concepts of independence and sharing of value, we would draw the line in the sand and they would back away. Our test was always, "Would the changes and structure proposed by the bureaucrats impact the basic philosophy we sought to implement?" If the answer was no, then we let them have their way. When the answer was yes, then we held firm. The result was that in the debates over the structure of AIMS, the bureaucrats won most of the battles, while we won the war.

The secret is that in most business situations you don't want to be the first one to put your position on the table, but when dealing with bureaucrats, the exact opposite is the best course of action. First of all they will be playing ice hockey in hell before a bureaucrat of any type will come forward with a plan. And even if they do, you will not be able to live with it. No, to have any chance of success battling the bureaucracy, you must have it responding to your plan. I have learned from experience that when dealing with bureaucrats, if you put the plan on the table you have an excellent chance to have your principles emerge intact and with 80 percent of what you recommend. And, believe it or not, the bureaucrats will think they won!

Bonus Secret 6: Entwine the Interests of the Organization with Your Efforts to the Point that It Becomes Impossible for Them to Stop You

You know the old saying that the best way to have a good relationship with a bank is to get so deep in debt to them that they can't afford to call the loans. The same philosophy is true when it comes to building an entrepreneurial culture within a bureaucratic organization. The more you are able to tie together the potential results of your effort with the potential benefit and needs of the organization, the more difficult it will be for the bureaucrats to stop you.

This secret applies all across the board, whether you are building an efficient entrepreneurial mailroom or a large independent operation such as we were with Allianz and AIMS.

At my first corporate job with State Mutual Insurance (now Allmerica), the bureaucrats were not especially happy with the way I was running my department or developing plans for what we call the "Total Living Concept." However, because sales had been down and the success of this plan was about the only chance the company had to turn things around, the bureaucrats had a very difficult time blocking my actions.

I had the same problem at ITT Life where the idea of turning ITT Life into an entrepreneurial culture did not sit very well with the bureaucrats at Hartford, who owned ITT. Yet, Hartford had an overriding desire to turn ITT Life around so it could be sold. If the actions we took in building an entrepreneurial ITT Life culture enhanced the value of the company, then so be it. The bureaucrats actually had little power to interfere with our efforts. Because ITT Life was to be eventually sold, Hartford did not have to worry about the entrepreneurial culture infecting the purity of the Hartford bureaucracy. (And trust me, Hartford Insurance was the purest of pure bureaucracies.)

The AIMS initiative is another example of the power of the secret of entwinement. The Allianz leaders recognized the lucrative potential of the retirement income market in North America and were hungry for a piece of the action. We are talking about billions of dollars of potential revenues here and once the Allianz leaders bought the idea that the only way they were going to pick the fruit in this market was by supporting the business model of AIMS, the bureaucrats were really powerless to stop the effort. Oh sure, they could obfuscate, probe, question, resist, and delay, but everyone knew there was no way they could stop the plan.

Bonus Secret 7: Don't Forget That Bureaucrats Never Give Up

Bureaucrats have nothing to do but be bureaucrats. If they stop trying to do nothing, they will have nothing to do. Never talk yourself into believing that you can ever eradicate bureaucracy. Bureaucrats are more dangerous than a jilted lover who works in a gun store. A good bureaucrat is nothing if not relentless. They have more resiliency and comeback power than anybody.

I have discovered that one of the first things a bureaucrat learns at Bureaucracy State University (BSU) is to repeat the bureaucrat's mantra: "Okay, we approve what you are doing, but we just need to make a few changes and everything will be fine."

Don't believe it.

Falling for that line is like going for a "sucker pin" on the golf course. It may look easy and appealing, but chances are that if you go for it you will end up in a trap. If I have heard that line once, I have heard it a thousand times and it is straight out of BSU.

Of course, what that line really means is that the bureaucrats have attacked your plan at one point and found stiff resistance, so they are going to back off and try another approach.

This brings up another little interesting secret about bureaucrats. They shy away from conflict and confrontation. They simply don't like it and will go to almost any cost to avoid being in such a situation. They are most comfortable working behind your back. This situation creates an advantage that entrepreneurs have over bureaucrats. A true entrepreneur has a passion and a commitment for the vision and the objective. This is a brand on the soul of the entrepreneur. The bureaucrat has no soul, no passion, and no commitment. The bureaucrat is loyal only to process and procedure and thus becomes uncomfortable in the presence of passion and performance.

This means that when it comes to the most critical issues of a project, the way for the entrepreneur to win is to go right at the bureaucrat—head on full force—with no backing down. Invariably the bureaucrat will fold his files and slink away. However, make no mistake: They will be back.

Countless times during the AIMS debate we would receive this "the plan is approved, but we just have to make a few changes" message. Those less experienced in the process reacted to these messages with a sense of victory and relief. More than a few times I heard, "Good, now that we have approval, we can move on to the important stuff." It made me feel like a parent telling a child that Santa Claus was not real when I informed my staff the battle was far from over. Sure enough, no sooner had "the plan been approved" when two or three more "issues" would sail over the transom. Of course, we were told that if these could be resolved then that would be the end of it. Fighting bureaucracy in this manner is like fighting a multiheaded monster. Cut off one head and two more pop out.

Even now, with AIMS moving forward "under full approval," we have to keep in mind that the battle is not over. As an entrepreneurial culture within a larger bureaucratic organization, we have to accept and understand that every action taken will cause an equal if not greater reaction from the bureaucrats. Running an entrepreneurial culture within a bureaucracy is like protecting an artificial beach from ocean erosion. The beach is beautiful, adds value, and people enjoy its benefits, but it has to be constantly tended and protected from attack.

You Can't Argue with a Winner

Of course, the best way to keep bureaucrats at bay is simple—be successful. An entrepreneurial culture inoculated with the serum of success is the ultimate immunity from the attacks of bureaucrats. They don't go away, but they become powerless to be anything more than a nuisance.

Back when we were in the early stages of developing LifeUSA, a bureaucratic organization—Transamerica—was in virtual control of the company. At almost every meeting, the bureaucrats would find something to attack or complain about. This was depressing for those of us attempting to move forward. Relying on my past experiences, I remember telling everyone, "Don't worry about it. Just keep doing what we are doing and as soon as we start having some success, they will go away." Fortunately, we did achieve success and my prediction became reality.

The same was true in my experience at ITT Life dealing with Hartford. After the effort was made to convert ITT Life into an entrepreneurial culture, we were under constant attack from the Hartford bureaucrats. However, as soon as sales and profits began to increase, the bureaucrats quickly lost influence.

This effect puts the bureaucrats in the ironic position of hoping that entrepreneurial efforts are not successful because success is the anathema to bureaucracy. But that only fends them off. They never quit trying and when the guard of success is dropped, they are back in force.

Where Do We Stand Now?

As the writing of this book concludes (June 2007), AIMS is up and operating as an independent company within the Allianz bureaucracy. About 30 individuals have eagerly left "secure" jobs with Allianz companies to take a risk and become entrepreneurs with AIMS. (It was encouraging that scores more than we needed came to AIMS looking for the opportunity!) Over 7,000 agents have signed on to be "partners" of AIMS. New systems are being developed for wireless and paperless processing. New products are being developed and sales are at a run rate of $100 million per year and growing rapidly.

These accomplishments have been achieved in the just 12 short months since AIMS opened for business and fully six months prior to actual approval from Allianz. These milestones would be remarkable for any start-up, but they must be considered exceptional in light of the bureaucratic environment of Allianz. I am also convinced we would still be "discussing" what should be done to enter the retirement market if the decision had been made to keep the effort within "the system." This early success is the result of being able to "beat the system."

To be fair, fighting through the Allianz bureaucracy has some trade-off value. Even though AIMS has been a start-up venture and despite the resistance from "the system," there are some unique advantages to building the culture under the Allianz umbrella. The platform provided by the reputation, credibility, and financial resources of a company such as Allianz has enabled AIMS to develop with the speed and efficiency of a start-up, yet present itself with the standing of an established organization.

While I am confident that with the business model and market opportunity of AIMS the company could be successful as a truly independent start-up company, there is no way the company could be as far along as it is today under such a scenario. If there is a lesson to be learned or irony here, it is that AIMS has the better of two worlds. The company is able to be independent and entrepreneurial while leaning on the credibility and financial support of a very bureaucratic organization. Another irony is that if AIMS is truly successful as an entrepreneurial company, the primary beneficiary of that success will be the bureaucratic Allianz. This could only have been accomplished by beating the system.

The success of AIMS is not yet assured. A lot of hard work and competition lies ahead. And the bureaucrats of Allianz have by no means surrendered. Many battles remain to be fought. However, that is not the point. What's important is that an entrepreneurial culture has been born within a bureaucratic organization. And that company has the opportunity to achieve remarkable success. As an entrepreneur, that is all you can ask for!

Epilogue: Certificate of Guaranteed Entrepreneurial Success

Be it known to all who have read this book that success as an entrepreneur is hereby and forever bestowed upon them and fully guaranteed. Elements of this guaranteed success include:

- Personal satisfaction with career accomplishments
- Enhanced leadership abilities
- High levels of trust and respect from others
- Significant reduction of risk in any business venture
- Increased opportunity to provide leadership
- Recognition as a problem solver

- The confidence to know what to do, when to do it, and how to do it
- The ability to make things happen
- The reputation as a "doer"
- Certification as an official bureaucracy beater

To maintain this guarantee in full force and effect, the reader agrees to the following conditions:

- Acceptance that the entrepreneurial secrets exposed in this book present a cohesive total *philosophy* for being an entrepreneur.
- A commitment to the implementation of the secrets with flawless ethics.
- Recognition that the entrepreneurial lifestyle espoused in this work is not mysterious or mystical but rather quite simple, basic, and fundamental.
- Appreciation of the reality that these secrets are interdependent and do not stand alone.
- Acknowledgment that becoming an entrepreneur is a lifetime all-or-nothing proposition.
- That implementation of the secrets is not a selective process and all secrets must be implemented in a coordinated fashion.
- A desire to see others benefit from your use of the secrets as much as you do.
- Recognition that the secrets are not magic pills or silver bullets. You are. But the secrets only work if you work them.
- That you teach the secrets to those you work with and encourage them to use the secrets.
- Understand that bureaucracy will never give up or give in and to beat it you must be committed and constantly vigilant.
- You must be willing to begin the process of becoming a successful entrepreneur immediately.

Beat the System was written to demonstrate that you can escape from the bonds of bureaucracy no matter where you are on the corporate ladder. This book is not intended to help you survive the bureaucracy, but to beat it and to thrive. I am hopeful it has shown you how to carve out your own path to entrepreneurial success by understanding what a true entrepreneur is all about—not that cardboard entrepreneur you learned about in college or business school.

I hope this book has helped you develop the critical awareness to begin your program of personal and professional assessment of where you are and what you want to accomplish. As noted earlier, the individual who develops an *awareness* of the bureaucratic rules that bind and limit our potential almost subconsciously and irresistibly develops an *interest* in breaking the rules and charting new, more entrepreneurial courses of action.

And that's the bottom line for this book: If you've come away from this work with the feeling that you can become an entrepreneur in the fullest sense of the word and are willing to make the personal changes to make that possible—terrific! Part of my mission has been achieved. If you're already started to make changes, that's even better. Just keep it going. But if you're still standing on the sidelines, get started—right now, *today*—and stick with it. These 11 secrets have worked for me and they have worked for others. I guarantee they will work for you.

Appendix: Sample Memo to the Gods

Memorandum

To: Jan Carendi
From: Bob MacDonald
Date: 4/28/06
Re: Decumulation Initiative—Structure and Funding Concepts
Jan,

The purpose of this memo is to outline various options available and to make a firm recommendation as to the structure of the proposed shared ownership concept for the Allianz "decumulation" initiative.

Using "shared ownership" is admittedly a radical departure from the traditional Allianz business model. However, if Allianz is committed to entering and ultimately leading the emerging income and legacy transfer market in the quickest, most efficient, effective, and lowest cost way, then the recommended approach should be adopted. And, equally important, the recommendation being made meets the objectives and answers the concerns of the involved parties.

There is also the potential that such an approach, if successful, could be adopted as a model for other Allianz AG projects.

Before the details are displayed it would be good to review the core operational philosophy that drives the concept of shared ownership. This philosophy is based on the belief that those who have the ability to add value to an organization will be encouraged to do so when they are allowed to share in the value created.

While there are multiple ways to achieve a "shared value" concept, the most efficient and effective structure is actual shared risk and ownership.

The proven motivation and powerful incentive created by the philosophy of "shared value" can be accomplished without the lead organization such as Allianz surrendering either financial or operational control.

There are three variations of shared ownership and value that could be adopted by Allianz to implement this concept. (Allianz will be used as a general term, but it could mean any Allianz entity, such as Allianz Life or Allianz of North America.)

(All figures are for example only and not intended to be actual.)

Scenario 1

Allianz forms a holding company—Allianz Income Life Holding Company (AILHC). The company is funded with $25.0 million. AILHC would issue 25.0 million shares of common stock to Allianz, creating a book value for the shares of $1.

The $25.0 million of invested capital would be used by AILHC to acquire an insurance company shell, possibly a broker dealer, and to build the infrastructure and distribution needed to penetrate the income and legacy market.

Allianz would enter into an agreement to sell up to 12.0 million shares of the stock it owns in AILHC to employees and agents of

AILHC. Employees and agents will be required to allocate 10 percent of their salary and commissions toward the purchase of AILHC stock from Allianz. The cost of the stock purchased by employees and agents would be at $1 per share or the current book value of the shares, whichever is higher.

The advantage gained from this approach is to put Allianz, employees and agents in perfect parallel when it comes to interest in the success of AILHC. What benefits one party benefits each party. The purchase of shares of AILHC (for the same cost as Allianz) provides employees and agents a method to share with Allianz in the value they create in the company, but they also, as with Allianz, risk their own capital in the effort.

In addition, this approach allows Allianz to immediately begin to reduce the cost of its capital investment in AILHC. The risk of loss and success is transferred and shared with employees and agents.

The difficulty with this approach is that it only transfers capital among and between Allianz, employees and agents, when, in reality, additional capital will be needed to fund the growth of AILHC. Once the initial $25.0 million has been invested, the question is where addition funds come from to support the growth of AILHC?

Scenario 2

As with Scenario 1, Allianz forms a holding company, funds it with $25.0 million of capital and receives 25.0 million shares of common stock. Initial capital is used to acquire a shell company and the infrastructure needed to underwrite and issue new policies. However, instead of Allianz selling the stock it owns to employees and agents, AILHC files a shelf registration of newly issued stock (thus becoming a public company) for 20.0 million shares and this stock is sold to employees and agents at a price of $1 per share or book value, whichever is higher.

This approach has the effect of diluting the Allianz interest (never below controlling) but does so by adding additional capital to AILHC, on the same or higher cost basis as the Allianz initial investment. Each time employees and agents purchase stock additional capital is contributed to the company.

This option is the purest form of "shared ownership and value" (it is the actual model LifeUSA followed), but—as with Scenario 1—it is complicated.

Thoughts . . .

Either of the two options would be very effective in achieving the objectives of the Allianz AG decumulation initiative to become a lead player in the income and legacy transfer market. In fact, they would both create an efficient, effective, and low cost path to success. However, there would be delay identifying and acquiring a shell insurance company, due to the radical nature of this business model in the Allianz system there may be uncertainty from Allianz AG Board of Management and ongoing governance and financial controls would be complicated.

As a result, I am going to recommend against either of the scenarios and propose a third alternative.

While this third scenario for "shared value" is not as pure as the two previously mentioned, it is a good compromise that will still achieve the objective of fast, efficient, effective, and low cost entry into the income and legacy market while being less radical in design and more palatable for the Allianz Board of Management.

In addition, this alternative will eliminate any appearance of conflict with Allianz Life and enable entrance into the market more rapidly and with less initial invested capital. This approach also has the benefit of a structure that converts most costs from a fixed to variable basis. That is, costs are, for the most part, based on successful activity only.

Proposal . . .

There is an established history of success for the proposed model.

Allianz Life would fund the formation of Allianz Income Management Company (AIMC). Rather than being formed as an insurance holding company, AIMC is actually formed as a combination of a marketing company, product developer, underwriter and third-party administrator. AIMC will provide all the marketing services of a marketing company and the administrative services of an insurance company, without actually being an insurance company.

(For those who know the history of the long term relationship between Allianz and LifeUSA, AIMC would act in the same relationship to (today's) Allianz Life as LifeUSA did when (the old) Allianz Life was "fronting" for LifeUSA in nine states. LifeUSA would perform all the functions of the "underwriter" yet the business would be issued on Allianz paper.)

AIMC would be formed by Allianz Life with say $10.0 million of capital contribution in exchange for 10.0 million shares of common stock. AIMC would then file a shelf registration for 10.0 million shares that would be sold to employees and agents (via salary or commission reduction) at $1 per share or book value, which ever is higher. (As employees and agents purchase increasing amounts of AIMC stock, Allianz Life would be given options to purchase additional amounts, at the same price, in order to maintain majority control.) Of course, purchases of stock by employees and agents reduces the amount of capital that would be required to be contributed by Allianz.

Employees will remain or be hired by Allianz Life and then "leased" to AIMC for a fee equal to the expense of each employee.

Remember, and this is critical to making the concept work, AIMC will perform all of the functions of an insurance company (just as LifeUSA did for old Allianz) with the exception that the policies marketed, issued, and administered by AIMC will be Allianz Life policies.

AIMC would be compensated by Allianz Life in two ways:

1. For the marketing and administrative services performed by AIMC a payment of a "policy acquisition, underwriting, and maintenance fee," priced into the product. Out of this fee AIMC would pay commissions, salaries, and expenses of the company and any remainder would flow to profit.

2. AIMC would share in the profits of a minimum of 25 percent of the business produced by AIMC, after the cost of capital has been deducted. For example, if new business written requires $10.0 million in capital, AIMC would be credited with 25 percent of the profits of the business, less the cost of capital for $2.5 million. (This percentage could vary depending on factors that can be discussed later.)

Thus, AIMC can become profitable—and the book value of the stock increase—if the company is successful in acquiring, issuing, and servicing the business for an amount less than the "service fee" paid by Allianz and if the business produced by AIMC is profitable for Allianz Life. (Remember Allianz Life will also receive at least 50 percent of all profits of AIMC right back into the company.)

Assuming no future IPO, Allianz Life could guarantee liquidity for employees and agents with the right to "put" the stock to Allianz after a period of time (say five years) at the then book value of AIMC. Allianz Life, after a like period of time, would have the right to "call" the stock in AIMC for the then book value, plus a premium. (Issues will have to be resolved regarding the stock of terminated, disabled, retired, or deceased employees and agents.)

This approach offers great advantages:

- It is very simple and easy to understand.
- Speed to market is dramatically improved as there is no need to take the time or invest the capital to acquire and license a life insurance company charter.
- Virtually all necessary forms, materials, and contracts are in place eliminating development and regulatory approval effort and time.
- Allianz Life (therefore Allianz) retains control of the entire effort.
- Having employees and agents share in the ownership of a subsidiary "marketing company" of Allianz Life should be much easier for members of the Allianz AG Board of Management to accept. (Such a situation actually exists today with the Allianz Life "project procures.")
- The capital needed to initiate the decumulation project is significantly reduced.
- Additional capital needed to write new business is placed only in Allianz Life (not a company with shared ownership) and only as new business demands it.
- Allianz AG governance and financial controls do not have to be duplicated, increasing reliability and reducing costs.
- If the project fails, the exit strategy is simplified.
- If the project is successful AIMC can be left independent, spun off in an IPO, or rolled back into and under Allianz Life.
- Employees and agents of AIMC are still in parallel with Allianz and have an investment in the company creating incentive for low cost, efficient operations and high quality, profitable business.
- This is the type of model that could easily be implemented in other Allianz AG operations.

Based on all the above factors, I believe we have the outline of a structure that will answer the questions and meet the needs of those interested in the decumulation project. And most important, this structure will enable early and quick entrance into the market coupled with proven incentive for employees and agents to work in parallel with Allianz to achieve success.

Index